THE
PASSION
TRANSLATION

Letters
OF
Love

FROM
PETER,
JOHN,
AND
JUDE

Translated from Greek and Aramaic Texts

DR. BRIAN SIMMONS

tPt
BIObE

BroadStreet
PUBLISHING

Letters of Love: From Peter, John, and Jude, The Passion Translation

Translated from Greek and Aramaic texts by Dr. Brian Simmons

Published by BroadStreet Publishing Group, LLC
Racine, Wisconsin, USA
BroadStreetPublishing.com

Copyright © 2016 The Passion Translation®

ISBN-13: 978-1-4245-5312-9 (paperback)
ISBN-13: 978-1-4245-5313-6 (e-book)

Cover design by Garborg Design Works, Inc. | garborgdesign.com
Interior typesetting by Katherine Lloyd | theDESKonline.com

Printed in the United States of America
16 17 18 19 20 5 4 3 2 1

TRIUMPHANT HOPE

Translator's Introduction to 1 Peter

AT A GLANCE

Author: The apostle Peter

Audience: Churches in Northwestern Asia Minor, modern Turkey

Date: AD 62–65

Type of Literature: A letter

Major Themes: God's nature, salvation, the church, the Christian life, and suffering

Outline:

Letter Opening — 1:1–2
Identity as God's Chosen People and Foreigners — 1:3–2:10
Living Honorably as Foreigners — 2:11–3:12
Responding to Hostility as Foreigners — 3:13–4:6
Living in Christian Solidarity as Foreigners — 2:1–22
Suffering Together as Foreigners — 3:1–13
Letter Closing — 3:14–18

ABOUT 1 PETER

Everyone needs grace to overcome life's hurdles. For some, they need to overcome a difficult marriage, or the frustration of children who have wandered away. For others it may be their limitations and hardships. First Peter is the book of strengthening grace and triumphant hope. There is an abundance of hopeful grace found within the verses of this book to set you free. You are a victorious overcomer, and God's grace is our fuel to empower our hearts to soar!

Peter was the first preacher to bring the gospel of Christ to the Jews in Jerusalem. At Pentecost he stood fearlessly and told the thousands gathered around him that they had denied the Holy One of God and crucified their Messiah. Yet just fifty days earlier, the apostle Peter, while Jesus was being tried by Pilate, denied that he even knew Jesus. Three times he succumbed to the weakness of his flesh. But Jesus had prophesied all this beforehand and gave him both a promise and a commission:

> "I have prayed for you, Peter, that you would stay faithful to me no matter what comes. Remember this: after you have turned back to me and have been restored, make it your life mission to strengthen the faith of your brothers." (Luke 22:32)

Jesus told Peter that his life mission after his resurrection would be to strengthen the faith of believers worldwide. So you will discover that there is an unusual grace upon Peter's letters (known as General Epistles) to strengthen you in your faith. Don't be surprised if after reading these letters you become emboldened to persevere, empowered to overcome, and encouraged to remain faithful to Christ. For the grace that restored Peter after his fall is also on Peter's letters to restore every believer and impart to them overcoming grace.

The Roman historian Eusebius informs us that Peter was crucified in Rome by Nero. The church tradition records that when Peter was being crucified, he pleaded with them to turn the cross upside down, stating that he was not worthy to be crucified in the same way as Jesus. Because of their respect for the godly Peter, the soldiers complied with his request. Peter turned the world upside down with the gospel power he carried, then he died on an upside-down cross. Peter experienced the triumph of grace. Our prayer for you is that the truth you read in the following pages will release within you this same amazing grace and triumphant hope!

PURPOSE

There is rich teaching found in 1 Peter, showing us that the community of Christ is a holy nation made up of kings and priests and lovers of God. And Peter teaches us the ways of purity and righteousness, and how to remain faithful to God all the days of our lives as members of a kingdom that chafes against the values of the world. He wrote this letter to Christians undergoing persecution for living in a way that was different than their unbelieving neighbors. His letter was meant to encourage them in their suffering and give it purpose as a vital aspect of Christian living.

This is a letter about God and living for him—no matter what the costs. Some of the themes of 1 Peter include holiness and being faithful in the midst of persecution. When others turn away from us, the presence of Christ grows stronger in our lives. It pushes our souls deeper into God's overcoming grace. No matter what you face and no matter what you may be passing through in your life today, there is a power from on high to make you into an overcomer. Let Peter's letter show you the way!

AUTHOR AND AUDIENCE

Written about AD 62 from "Babylon" (a cryptic term for Rome), Peter longed to encourage and strengthen the faith of those who were being persecuted for following Christ. Although Aramaic was his first language, the fisherman Peter's refined use of Greek has caused some scholars to even doubt that he wrote this first epistle. We do know however that every good writer has a brilliant editor. Peter's editor for this letter was Silvanus (5:12), who no doubt helped Peter with the more elegant Greek words (much like the vocabulary of Paul), which are found in these five chapters.

Peter was the first missionary to go to the Gentiles. After a divine trance he experienced on the rooftop in Joppa, Peter took the keys of the kingdom and opened the door of faith for the Gentiles. He broke the religious limitation that the gospel was only meant for the Jews. Peter found his way to the house of Cornelius, a Roman Gentile, and he and all his family became followers of Jesus. He continued this mission by writing to Christians living in the Roman regions of Northeastern Asia Minor (modern-day Turkey), to encourage them in their suffering; provoke holy living and growth in God; and explain their new birth through Christ's blood. We all have a debt of love to the apostle Peter. Enjoy his letter as you read it with an open and thankful heart.

MAJOR THEMES

God the Father, God the Son, God the Holy Spirit. Who God is and what God is like is front and center in Peter's letter, because all of the teachings relate to him in some way. He's referred to as "Father God" or "God the Father," which should tell us something about how we encounter him: as a Father! He's also described as the mighty and powerful Creator and Judge, but also as our merciful and gracious Redeemer.

Of course as Redeemer, the Son of God is also featured prominently in this letter. One of the most important names Peter uses for Jesus is "Anointed One." This is a deeply Hebrew idea for the Messiah, the One whom God the Father destined "before the foundation of the world was laid" to be sacrificed for us "like a spotless, unblemished lamb." It is this suffering that forms the basis for his saving work; our salvation was achieved through his crucifixion! While Jesus was fully revealed while he was on earth, he will be ultimately revealed on the last day, bringing with him the full revelation of our salvation and God's grace.

Then there is the Holy Spirit, who is vital for our ongoing Christian life, for a number of reasons: he's the one who has set us apart to be God's holy ones in the first place; he is the source of the gospel revelation, which goes out from us and draws people into God's family; and he lives in us to help us obey God as his chosen ones. Peter unveils before us the revelation-truth that he is our power as we live in this world as resident aliens and foreigners, awaiting Christ's return when he comes to make all things new.

The Nature of Our Salvation. Peter uses a number of images and words to convey to his readers the breadth and depth of their salvation in Jesus Christ. Followers of Christ have been "gloriously sprinkled with his blood" (1:2); have been redeemed once and for all through the precious blood of Christ (1:18–19); have been purified through obedience (1:22); have tasted "of the goodness of the Lord Jehovah and have experienced his kindness" (2:3); have been brought near to God (3:18).

This language reflects two ways in which believers have been changed: through Christ's sacrifice, and being born again. First, Peter uses sacrificial metaphors to explain what's happened to us. These are drawn from the ancient temple cultic practices of blood-shedding and purification. Second, Peter explains our salvation is a "new birth" into a new family, and we've inherited all of the benefits of that royal birth. So when we say we've been "born again," we are reflecting the language that Peter himself used to talk about what's happened to us!

Life in God's Family as a Spiritual "Nation." The inevitable outgrowth of our salvation and new birth in Christ is a new way of living and in concert with our new family and a spiritual "nation." We are to practice hope and holiness, fear of God, and growth in the knowledge of God. The reason why we devote ourselves to these pursuits is because we've been bought by the blood of Jesus. Without this new birth, there is no reason to obey; without the hope of salvation the Christian life is pointless.

What's interesting about Peter's letter is that he doesn't envision this kind of life as a solitary endeavor. Life in God's family is just that: a family affair! First, those in God's family are described as being "chosen" and "elect," which recalls the story of ancient Israel. This is intentional, as the church is the continuation and culmination of Israel as the new, true people of God. This idea frames the whole letter, appearing in the first verse and the last. They are the ones who've received God's grace and favor.

Not only are those in this community chosen and elect, they are also family. Being the household of God frames this letter as much as being chosen and elected. It also frames how we are to live: we are to live as "obedient children" (1:14); we are to be holy as the Father is holy; we are to live within a new familial structure, accepting the authority of elders; and we are to love one another as siblings, wrapping ourselves with "the apron of a humble servant" (5:5).

Suffering and Persecution. Inevitably, when we live as obedient children of God, and the believing community takes seriously its role as "priests who are kings, a spiritual 'nation' set apart as God's devoted ones" (2:9), there's going to be conflict with the surrounding world. But Peter wants believers, who are "resident aliens and foreigners in this world" (2:11), to take heart: "the grief of so many trials...reveal the sterling core of your faith" (1:7). Persecution is a refiner's fire that unfolds the brilliance of authentic faith. And when we do suffer for Christ, Jesus is praised, glorified, and honored. Ultimately, persecution is a privilege, for we "carry the Anointed One's name!" (4:16). God will never fail those who suffer for him!

One

Our Living Hope

[1]From Peter, an apostle of Jesus the Anointed One, to the chosen ones[a] who have been scattered abroad like "seed" into the nations living as refugees,[b] to those living in Pontus,[c] Galatia, Cappadocia,[d] and throughout *the Roman provinces of* Asia and Bithynia.[e] [2]*You are not forgotten,* for you have been chosen and destined by Father God. The Holy Spirit has set you apart to be God's holy ones, obedient followers of Jesus Christ who have been *gloriously* sprinkled with his blood. May God's delightful grace and peace cascade over you many times over![f]

[3]Celebrate with praises the God and Father of our Lord Jesus Christ, who has shown us his extravagant mercy. For his *fountain of* mercy has given us a new life—we are reborn[g] to experience a living, energetic hope[h] through the resurrection of Jesus Christ from the dead.[i] [4]We are reborn into a perfect

---

a 1:1 Or "elect (believers)." As God's chosen people, this would also refer to the faithful within unfaithful Israel.

b 1:1 First Peter, Hebrews, and James were all written to believers who had been scattered like seed among the nations due to persecution. *Exile* is the way the original audience would have described the situation in their day. *Refugee* is a modern equivalent in ours.

c 1:1 Pontus is the region of the Turkish coast of the Black Sea.

d 1:1 Galatia and Cappadocia are regions of central Turkey.

e 1:1 The provinces of Asia (Minor) and Bithynia are modern western Turkey.

f 1:2 Or "be multiplied to you." Notice all three members of the Trinity are mentioned in this verse: Father God, the Holy Spirit, and Jesus Christ. We are chosen by the Father, set apart (or sanctified) by the Holy Spirit, and submitted to Christ.

g 1:3 This is the only place in the New Testament where the Greek verb *anagennaō* is found (hapax legomenon). This shows that God himself is the one who "begets us" as newborn believers filled with the life of Christ. God is truly our Father, who gave us new life through his living mercy.

h 1:3 Some Greek manuscripts and the Aramaic read "the hope of life."

i 1:3 Peter states that the first result of our new birth is that we are brought into a living hope in the power of God, based on the resurrection of Christ. The God of resurrection gives us a powerful hope to excel in life.

inheritance[a] that can never perish, never be defiled, and never diminish. It is promised and preserved forever in the heavenly realm for you![b]

[5]Through our faith, the mighty power of God constantly guards[c] us until our *full* salvation[d] is ready to be revealed[e] in the last time. [6]May the thought of this cause you to jump for joy,[f] even though lately you've had to put up with the grief of many trials.[g] [7]But these only reveal the sterling core[h] of your faith, which is far more valuable than gold that perishes, for even gold is refined by fire. *Your authentic faith* will result in even more praise, glory, and honor when Jesus the Anointed One is revealed.[i]

[8]You love him passionately although you did not see him, but through believing in him you are saturated with an ecstatic joy, indescribably sublime and immersed in glory.[j] [9]For you are reaping the harvest of your faith—the full salvation promised you—your souls' victory![k]

---

a 1:4 The second result that comes from our new birth is an eternal inheritance, which is available now, by faith, and will also be reserved in heaven for us when we pass from death to life. Paul describes it as *"every spiritual blessing"* that has already been given to us (Eph. 1:3).

b 1:4 This would no doubt encourage those believers who had scattered from their homelands and been deprived of what they once possessed. Their blessings (and ours) are not material, but spiritual, from a transcendent reality.

c 1:5 The Greek word for "guards us" is *phrouroumenous,* which comes from a military term (*phrouria*) meaning "a fort" or "an army garrison stationed to defend a city." You are continually being watched over and protected by God's mighty power.

d 1:6 The third result of our new birth that Peter mentions is our full salvation (or deliverance) that will come when Christ is unveiled. It is ready to be revealed and waits for our discovery.

e 1:5 The Greek verb *apokalyptō* means "to unveil and disclose." Peter is saying that there is a more complete salvation awaiting us when Christ is unveiled in the last days. The nominalized form of *apokalyptō* is the title of the last book of the Bible, The Revelation (Unveiling) of Jesus Christ. In just a few verses Peter will tell us that a "grace" will also be revealed to us in the last days (1:13).

f 1:6 Or "exult in joy." The Aramaic is "rejoice for eternity."

g 1:6 Peter speaks of believers suffering difficulties and persecutions four times in his first letter (1:6–7; 3:13–17; 4:12–19; 5:9).

h 1:7 Or "proven character."

i 1:7 Or "comes out of his concealment."

j 1:8 The Aramaic can be translated "a glorification that cannot be described."

k 1:9 Or "the salvation of your souls."

Overcoming Grace

[10]This salvation was the focus of the prophets who prophesied of this *outpouring of* grace that was destined for you. They made a careful search and investigation of the meaning *of their God-given prophecies* [11]as they probed into *the mysteries* of who would fulfill them and the time period when it would all take place. The Spirit of the Anointed One was in them[a] and was pointing prophetically to the sufferings that Christ was destined to suffer and the glories that would be released afterward. [12]God revealed to the prophets that their ministry was not for their own benefit[b] but for yours. And now, you have heard these things from the evangelists[c] who preached the gospel to you through *the power of* the Holy Spirit sent from heaven—the gospel *containing wonderful mysteries* that even the angels long to get a glimpse of.[d]

A Call to Holiness

[13]So then, prepare your *hearts and* minds for action![e] Stay alert and fix your hope firmly on the marvelous grace that is coming to you. For when Jesus Christ is unveiled,[f] *a greater measure of* grace will be released to you. [14]As God's obedient children, never again shape your lives by the desires that you

---

a 1:11 The Spirit of Christ was in the prophets of the Old Testament. This means that Enoch, Abraham, Jacob, Moses, Elijah, Elisha, Isaiah, Jeremiah, and all the prophets who prophesied did so by the Holy Spirit living in them. Today every believer has the Holy Spirit within him or her and everyone may prophesy. See Romans 8:9; 1 Corinthians 12 and 14.

b 1:12 That is, the prophets understood that their prophecies were not only for their generation but for generations to come.

c 1:12 The Aramaic is "extenders of hope."

d 1:12 Heavenly angels are fascinated with God's mercy shown toward us. His wise plan of making former rebels into lovers has mystified the angelic realm. The church is the University of Angels and every believer a professor. Angels long to peer into the mysteries of God's grace, which have been lavished upon us. How much more should we be fascinated explorers of the mercy of God, for we have received it and are now redeemed. See also Ephesians 3:10.

e 1:13 We would say today, "Roll up your sleeves," or, "Fasten your seat belt!"

f 1:13 Or "to come out of concealment, appear, be made manifest, revealed." Peter uses the Greek word *apokàlypsis,* which is the title of the last book in the Bible, The Revelation of Jesus Christ. The Aramaic can be translated "Stay alert and share the news about the joy that came to you with the revelation of Jesus the Messiah."

followed when you didn't know better. [15]Instead, shape your lives to become like the Holy One who called you. [16]For Scripture says:

You are to be holy, because I am also holy.[a]

[17]Since you call on him as your heavenly Father, the impartial Judge who judges according to each one's works,[b] live each day with holy awe and reverence throughout your time on earth.[c] [18]For you know that your lives were ransomed once and for all from the empty and futile way of life handed down from generation to generation. It was not a ransom payment of silver and gold, which eventually perishes, [19]but the precious blood of Christ—who like a spotless, unblemished lamb was *sacrificed for us.*[d]

[20]*This was part of God's plan*, for he was chosen and destined for this before the foundation of the earth was laid,[e] but he has been made manifest in these last days for you. [21]It is through him that you now believe in God,[f] who raised him from the dead and glorified him,[g] so that you would fasten your faith and hope in God *alone.*

---

a 1:16 See Leviticus 11:44 and 19:2. Everything about God is holy. True holiness includes justice, mercy, truth, and righteousness. To be holy is to be absolutely devoted to God in all that we do, demonstrating who he is to the world. Holiness surrounds God's throne and we are seated with him in heavenly places (Eph. 2:6). The Hebraic concept of holiness is "set apart"; that is, we are a people set apart for God, even as God is "set apart" from all gods. Grace has imbedded holiness into our lives, yet we are to make right choices and to yield to Christ and God's Word as the Holy Spirit lives in us. Holiness is not merely actions we perform, but what we absorb and manifest as we live our lives in God's presence. Christ is our holiness (1 Cor. 1:30).

b 1:17 The Aramaic is "No one will put on a face mask before him." Believers in Jesus will not be judged for their sins, since that happened once and for all when Jesus was crucified to redeem us. We will be judged, however, for our works in order to determine the reward (or lack of reward) that God gives to those who believe in Christ. See Isaiah 53:4–5; 1 Peter 2:24; Romans 14:10–12; 1 Corinthians 3:12–15.

c 1:17 Or "throughout the time of your exile."

d 1:19 See Exodus 12; Leviticus 22:20–25; Isaiah 53:7; John 1:29; Hebrews 4:15; 7:26–27.

e 1:20 Or "before the fall of the world." The Greek word *kataboles* can possibly mean "lay a foundation," or "a fall," or "casting down." See also Ephesians 1:4.

f 1:21 Or "You believe in him."

g 1:21 As translated from the Aramaic. The Greek is "and gave him glory."

Love and Purity

²²Now, because of your obedience to the truth,ᵃ you have purified your very souls, and this empowers you to be full of love for your fellow believers. So express this sincere love toward one another passionately and with a pure heart.ᵇ ²³For through the eternal and living Word of Godᶜ you have been born again. And this "seed" that he planted within you can never be destroyed but will live *and grow* inside of you forever. For:

> ²⁴**Human beings**ᵈ **are** *frail and temporary,* **like grass,**
> **and the glory of man** *fleeting*
> **like blossoms of the field.**ᵉ
> **The grass dries and withers and the flowers fall off,**
> ²⁵**but the Word of the Lord endures forever!**ᶠ

And this is the Wordᵍ that was announced to you!

---

a 1:22 Most later manuscripts have "through the Spirit." It is generally recognized by scholars today that this was likely an addition to the text.

b 1:22 This verse is packed with the virtues that should be seen in the lives of believers: obedience, truth, purification of our souls, authentic (sincere) love, fervent (passionate) expressions of love, and heart purity.

c 1:23 Or "the Word of the living and enduring God."

d 1:24 Or "All flesh."

e 1:24 As translated from the Aramaic.

f 1:24 See Isaiah 40:6–8.

g 1:24 As translated from the Aramaic. This reveals that Jesus is the Word proclaimed to the world. See John 1:1. The Greek is "This is the good news announced to you."

Two

Growing in Holiness

[1]So abandon[a] every form of evil, deceit, hypocrisy,[b] feelings of jealousy and slander. [2]In the same way that nursing infants cry for milk, you must intensely crave the pure[c] spiritual milk *of God's Word*.[d] For this "milk" will cause you to grow into maturity, fully nourished and strong for life[e]—[3]especially now that you have had a taste of the goodness of the Lord Jehovah and have experienced his kindness.[f]

[4]So keep coming to him who is the Living Stone[g]—though he was rejected and discarded by men but chosen by God and is priceless in God's sight. [5]Come and be his "living stones"[h] who are continually being assembled into a sanctuary for God. For now you *serve as* holy priests,[i] offering

---

a 2:1 Or "rid yourselves." The Aramaic uses an interesting word that could be translated "oasis rest." The thought is that we must be completely free from evil and be at rest within. Purity is an oasis rest for the people of God.

b 2:1 The Greek word *hupokrisis* (the behavior of a hypocrite) can also be translated "a hypercritical attitude of pulling things apart for judgmental analysis." The Aramaic is "wearing a face mask."

c 2:2 Or "unadulterated, guileless milk." The nourishment contained in the milk of the Word is like an antibiotic for guile. This milk contains an element that can eliminate our guile. Therefore, the Word is guileless, unadulterated milk.

d 2:2 Implied by the Greek word for "spiritual" (*logikos*), which seems to be a play on words with what Peter says in 1:23–25 concerning the living Word (*logos*) of God. The *pure spiritual milk* is the sustaining power of God's Word, coming from his very breast, as it were, to nourish and strengthen our inner being. From verse 3 we can see that this "milk" is the Lord himself dispensed to us in the Word of God. Our craving for this "milk" is not only because of necessity but of delight. He is the Seed, the Word, the Milk, the Lord, and the Living Stone.

e 2:2 As translated from the Aramaic. The Greek is "grow into salvation."

f 2:3 See Psalm 34:8 and Luke 1:53.

g 2:4 The church is built on Christ, "the Living Stone." See Psalm 118:22 and Isaiah 28:16.

h 2:5 To be identified as Christ's living stones means that we are in union with him and share his nature, for he is the Living Stone.

i 2:5 Or "priesthood (community of priests)." See Revelation 1:6; 5:10; 20:4–6.

up spiritual sacrifices that he readily accepts through Jesus Christ. [6]For it says in Scripture:

> **Look! I lay a cornerstone in Zion,**[a]
> **a chosen and priceless stone!**
> **And whoever believes in him**
> **will certainly not be disappointed.**[b]

[7]As believers you know his great worth—indeed, his preciousness is *imparted* to you.[c] But for those who do not believe:

> **The stone that the builders rejected and discarded**
> **Has now become the cornerstone**[d]

[8]And

> **A stone that makes them stumble**
> **And a rock to trip over.**[e]

They keep stumbling over the message because they refuse to believe it. And this they were destined to do. [9]But you are God's chosen treasure[f]—

---

a 2:6 Mount Zion was once a Jebusite stronghold conquered by David (2 Sam. 5:6–9), who made it the capital for his kingdom. This is inside the walls of present-day Jerusalem. Zion is used in both the Old and New Testaments as more than a location. Zion is referred to as the place of God's dwelling (Ps. 9:11; 48:1–2; 74:2; Isa. 8:18). God's people are called "the daughters of Zion" (Song 3:11; Zech. 9:9; John 12:15). Zion is the heavenly realm where God is manifest (Ps. 84:7; 102:16; 110:1–2; Heb. 12:22; Rev. 14:1).

b 2:6 Or "put to shame." See Isaiah 28:16.

c 2:7 Or "Unto you who believe is the preciousness." That is, all that Jesus is before the Father has now been transferred into our account. We stand before the Father in the "preciousness" of the Son. You are as precious to God as Jesus Christ is.

d 2:7 Or "capstone." See Psalm 118:22; Matthew 21:42; Mark 12:10; Luke 20:17; Acts 4:11.

e 2:8 Or "a rock of scandal." The Greek word *skandalon* means "a trap stick." See Isaiah 8:14.

f 2:9 This is taken from Exodus 19:5–6 and Malachi 3:17. The Hebrew word is *ségulla*, which means "a special treasure (possession)." It is used to describe "guarded wealth," indicating the placement of the king's jewels, treasures, etc. in a safe, protected place priests who are kings,[a] a spiritual "nation" set apart as God's devoted ones. He called you out of darkness to experience his marvelous light, and now he claims you as his very own. He did this so that you would broadcast his glorious wonders *throughout the world*.[b] [10]For at one time you were not God's people, but now you are. At one time you knew nothing of God's mercy, because you hadn't received it yet, but now you are drenched with it![c]

Living Godly Lives

[11]My divinely loved friends, since you are resident aliens and foreigners in this world, I appeal to you to divorce yourselves from the evil desires that wage war within you.[d] [12]Live honorable lives as you mix with unbelievers, even though they accuse you of being evildoers. For they will see your beautiful works and have a reason to glorify God in the day he visits us.[e]

[13]In order to honor the Lord, you must respect and defer to the authority of every human institution,[f] whether it be the highest ruler[g] [14]or the governors he puts in place to punish lawbreakers and to praise those who do what's right. [15]For it is God's will for you to silence the ignorance of foolish people[h] by doing what is right.

---

because of their extraordinary value. God says that each believer is a priest and king, his unique and special treasure of great importance—a treasure above all other treasures. See also Titus 2:14.

a 2:9 The nouns are in apposition ("a group of kings, a priesthood" or "a king's household, a priesthood"). There are other possible ways to translate this, such as "a priesthood of kings" or "a kingdom of priests."

b 2:9 See Isaiah 42:12 LXX and 43:20–21 LXX, where it is translated as "praises" or "worship." The Greek can also be translated "God's excellences (virtues)" or "wonders."

c 2:10 Or, in Aramaic, "mercies cascade over you." See Hosea 1:6; 9; 2:23. Both Israel and the church have been divinely chosen and showered with mercy.

d 2:11 Or "that wage war against your soul."

e 2:12 See Matthew 5:16; 18:20.

f 2:13 Or "every authority instituted by men." The Aramaic is "Submit to all the sons of men."

g 2:13 Or "emperor." At the time Peter wrote this letter, the Roman emperor was the infamous Nero, known for his tyranny and corruption.

h 2:15 That is, the unbelievers. The Aramaic makes it even more explicit: "the foolish who do not know God."

¹⁶As God's *loving* servants, you should live in complete freedom, but never use your freedom as a cover-up for evil. ¹⁷Recognize the value of every person and continually show love to every believer. Live your lives with great reverence and in holy awe of God. Honor your rulers.

The Example of Christ's Sufferings

¹⁸Those who are servants,ᵃ submit toᵇ the authority of those who are your masters—not only to those who are kind and gentle but even to those who are hard and difficult. ¹⁹You find God's favor by deciding to please God even when you endure hardships because of unjust suffering. ²⁰For what merit is it to endure mistreatment for wrongdoing? Yet if you are mistreated when you do what is right, and you faithfully endure it, this is commendable before God. ²¹In fact, you were called to live this way, because Christ also suffered in your place, leaving you his example for you to follow.

> ²²**He never sinned**
> **and he never spoke deceitfully** ᶜ

²³When he was verbally abused, he did not return with an insult; when he suffered, he would not threaten retaliation.ᵈ Jesus faithfully entrusted himself into the hands of God, who judges righteously. ²⁴**He himself carried our sins**ᵉ in his body on the cross ᶠ so that we would be dead to sinᵍ and live for righteousness. **Our instant healing flowed from his wounding.**ʰ ²⁵**You were**

---

a 2:18 Or "slaves."

b 2:18 The Greek word *hupotasso* means "to support, uphold, be under (authority)."

c 2:22 See Isaiah 53:9.

d 2:23 See Isaiah 53:7.

e 2:24 See Isaiah 53:4; 12.

f 2:24 Or "the tree."

g 2:24 The Greek word *apoginomai*, a hapax legomenon, means "to die" or "die to something." Although not the usual word for "to die," Peter is using this metaphorically for "dying to sin."

h 2:24 This healing includes the body, soul, and emotions. It was fulfilled in two ways: first, by the healing ministry of Jesus, and second, by the blood of Christ's wounds. See Matthew 8:16–17 and Isaiah 53:5.

like sheep that continually wandered away,[a] but now you have returned to the *true* Shepherd of your lives—the *kind* Guardian who *lovingly* watches over your souls.

Three

The Marriage Relationship

[1]And now let me speak to the wives. Be devoted to your own husbands,[b] so that even if some of them do not obey the Word of God, your kind conduct may win them over without you saying a thing. [2]For when they observe your pure, godly life before God, *it will impact them deeply.* [3-4]Let your true beauty come from your inner personality, not a focus on the external. For lasting beauty comes from a gentle and peaceful spirit, which is precious in God's sight *and is much more important* than the outward adornment of elaborate hair, jewelry,[c] and fine clothes.

[5]Holy women of long ago who had set their hopes in God beautified themselves with lives lived in deference to their own husbands' authority. [6]For example, our *"mother,"* Sarah, devoted herself[d] to her husband, Abraham, and even called him "master." And you have become her daughters when you do what is right without fear and intimidation.[e]

[7]Husbands, you in turn must treat your wives with tenderness,[f] view-

---

a 2:25 See Isaiah 53:6.

b 3:1 As translated from the Aramaic. The Greek is "defer to the authority of your husbands (patiently accept, submit)."

c 3:3-4 Or "braiding of hair or gold ornaments."

d 3:6 As translated from the Aramaic. The Greek is "obeyed."

e 3:6 That is, the wife is not inferior and should never be intimidated by her husband. The Aramaic is "without being terrified by any fear."

f 3:7 Or "with intimate insight (realistically, with considerateness)." That is, with consideration of what they desire and delight in, not ignorant of their preferences.

ing them[a] as feminine[b] partners who deserve to be honored, for they are co-heirs with you of the "*divine* grace of life,"[c] so that nothing will hinder your prayers.

Love One Another

[8]Now, this is the goal: to live in harmony with one another and demonstrate affectionate love,[d] sympathy,[e] and kindness toward other believers. Let humility describe who you are as you dearly love one another. [9]Never retaliate when someone treats you wrongly, nor insult those who insult you, but instead, respond by speaking a blessing over them—because a blessing is what God promised to give you.[f] [10]For the Scriptures tell us:

> **Whoever wants to embrace true life**
> **and find beauty in each day**
> **[11]must stop speaking evil, hurtful words**
> **and never deceive in what they say.**
> **Always turn from what is wrong**
> **and cultivate what is good;**
> **eagerly pursue peace in every relationship,**
> **making it your prize.**

---

a 3:7 Or "make a home as equals."

b 3:7 Or "weaker vessel," which is a possible idiom for "weaker livelihood." Widows and female orphans were horribly disadvantaged in the time this was written. Without an advocate, women were often oppressed by corrupt political officials. Peter instructs married men to treat their wives with respect, as those who are often disadvantaged. It is also possible to interpret this as weaker physically.

c 3:7 This unique New Testament phrase describes the joyous grace that husband and wife share as a married couple, as co-heirs of eternal life. But there is more than a hint of the life they give birth to—that is, the wonderful grace of giving life to a child, *the divine grace of life.*

d 3:8 Or "brotherly love."

e 3:8 The Aramaic is "Suffer with those who are suffering."

f 3:9 Every believer is blessed by God. There are eight virtues found in verses 8–9 that should characterize our fellowship as believers who follow Christ: 1) a sublime harmony, 2) demonstration of affectionate (brotherly) love, 3) sympathy, 4) kindness, 5) humility, 6) fervent love, 7) never retaliating evil for evil or insult for insult, 8) speaking blessings over those who mistreat us.

¹²**For the eyes of the Lord Yahweh**^a **rest upon the godly,**
and his heart responds to their prayers.
But he turns his back on those who practice evil.^b

Persecuted for Doing Good

¹³Why would anyone harm^c you if you're passionate and devoted^d to pleasing God? ¹⁴But even if you happen to suffer for doing what is right, you will have the *joyful* experience of the blessing of God.^e

And

Don't be intimidated or terrified
by those who would terrify you.^f

¹⁵But give reverent honor in your hearts to the Anointed One and treat him as the holy Master^g *of your lives*. And if anyone asks^h about the hope living within you, always be ready to explain your faith ¹⁶with gentleness and respect. Maintain a clean conscience, so that those who slander you for living a pure life in Christ will have to lie about you and will be ashamed because of their slander.ⁱ ¹⁷For it is better to suffer for doing good, if it is in God's plan, than for doing evil.

---

a 3:12 As translated from the Aramaic. The Greek is *kurios* (lord).

b 3:12 Or "He sets his face against evildoers." See Psalm 34:12–16.

c 3:13 The Aramaic is "do evil to you."

d 3:13 Or "eager to do good." The Aramaic word used for "passionate and devoted" is a homonym that can also mean "imitators." For this reason some Greek manuscripts have "followers/imitators of what is good."

e 3:14 There are three things to remember when you suffer mistreatment or persecution for the cause of Christ: 1) The eyes of God rest upon you, verse 12; 2) God's heart responds to your prayers, verse 12; 3) You will experience the blessing of God in spite of your enemies, with nothing to fear, verse 14.

f 3:14 As translated from the Aramaic. See Isaiah 8:12–13.

g 3:15 The Aramaic is "Lord Yahweh." This is a clear statement that Christ is the Lord Yahweh.

h 3:15 Or "repeatedly asks."

i 3:16 Or "be ashamed when they accuse you." We cannot prevent people from slandering us, but when they do, they should be forced to lie.

Christ's Victory

[18]Christ suffered and died[a] for sins once and for all—the innocent for the guilty[b]—to bring you near to God by his body[c] being put to death and by being raised to life by the Spirit. [19]He went in the spiritual realm[d] and made a proclamation to the spirits in prison[e] [20]because of their disobedience of long ago.[f] For during the time of Noah God patiently waited while the ark was being prepared, but only a few were brought safely through the floodwaters: a total of eight souls. [21]This was a prophetic picture[g] of the immersion that now saves you—not a bathing of the physical body but rather the response of a good conscience before God[h] through the resurrection of Jesus Christ, [22]who is now in heaven at the place of supreme authority next to God.[i] The very powers of heaven, including every angel and authority, now yield in submission to him.

---

a 3:18 There is great variation among reliable texts of this phrase. Some have "Christ suffered," and others read "Christ died." The translation has included both concepts.

b 3:18 Or "the just for the unjust." See Isaiah 53:11-12.

c 3:18 Or "by being put to death in/by the flesh." The passive verb ("having been put to death") implies that this was something done to him "by flesh (humanity)." The contrast is this: humanity put him on the cross, but the Spirit raised him up to life.

d 3:19 Or "through the (Holy) Spirit."

e 3:19 The Aramaic is "Sheol (Hades)." The Aramaic adds the clause "in hopes of their repentance," which is not found in the Greek.

f 3:19 The early church fathers cited this passage, along with others, in the belief that Jesus "descended into hell" (e.g., the Apostles' Creed, although the earliest versions of it do not include the words "descended into hell"). In this context, between his death and resurrection, Jesus is said to have gone into the underworld and preached (the victory of the cross) to the spirits (fallen angels) who are bound. See also Genesis 6:1-4; 2 Peter 2:4. However, Augustine, Aquinas, and others argue that the proclamation Jesus made was through Noah by the Holy Spirit to the people of Noah's day who were disobedient. Nearly every scholar concludes that this passage in 1 Peter is one of the most difficult in the New Testament to interpret.

g 3:21 The Greek word antitypos means "a picture, a type, a symbol, a pattern, or a counterpart."

h 3:21 Or "by the response of a good conscience." The word often translated "conscience" (syneidēsis) actually means "a joint knowing, a virtuous co-knowledge, or co-perception."

i 3:22 Or "at the right hand of God."

Four

Living in the Grace of God

[1]Since Christ, *though innocent,* suffered in his flesh for you,[a] now you also must be a prepared soldier,[b] having the same mind-set,[c] for whoever has died in his body is done with sin.[d] [2]So live the rest of your earthly life no longer concerned with human desires but *consumed* with what brings pleasure to God. [3]For you have already spent enough time doing what unbelievers[e] love to do—living in debauchery, sensuality, partying, drunkenness, wild drinking parties,[f] and the worship of demons.[g] [4]They marvel that you no longer rush to join them in the excesses of their corrupt lifestyles, and so they vilify you. [5]But one day they will have to give an account to the one who is destined to judge the living and the dead. [6]This is the reason the gospel was preached to the *martyrs before they gave their lives.*[h] Even though they were judged by human standards, now they live in spirit by God's standards.

---

a 4:1 As translated from the Aramaic and most Greek manuscripts. A few Greek manuscripts have "for us," while some reliable Greek texts read simply, "Christ suffered in his flesh." Variants of both the Greek and Aramaic text read, "Christ died for us."

b 4:1 The Greek word *hoplisasthe,* a hapax legomenon, means "to arm yourself" (like a foot soldier). It is used metaphorically to describe the battle we experience for moral purity in a decadent world. See also 1 Peter 2:11.

c 4:1 Or "attitude." That is, learn to think like him. The Aramaic can be translated "You also are nourished by him as you mediate on these things."

d 4:1 As translated from the Aramaic. The Greek is "For the one who suffers in the flesh is done with sin." See Romans 6:7.

e 4:3 Or "Gentiles."

f 4:3 Or "orgies."

g 4:3 As translated from the Aramaic. The Greek is "idolatries."

h 4:6 Or "to those who are dead." Most scholars believe that this refers to those who heard the gospel and eventually suffered and died for Christ. However, some believe it is preaching to the dead (the entire human family), giving them the opportunity to believe.

Prayer, Love, and Gifts of Grace

[7]Since we are approaching the end of all things, be intentional, purposeful,[a] and self-controlled so that you can be given to prayer.

[8]Above all, constantly echo[b] God's intense love for one another, for **love will be a canopy over a multitude of sins.**[c]

[9]Be compassionate to foreigners[d] without complaining.

[10]Every believer has received grace gifts, so use them to serve one another as faithful stewards of the many-colored tapestry of God's grace.

[11]*For example,* if you have a speaking *gift,* speak as though God were speaking his words through you.[e] If you have *the gift of* serving, do it *passionately* with the strength God gives you,[f] so that in everything God *alone* will be glorified through Jesus Christ. For to him belong the power and the glory forever throughout all ages! Amen.[g]

Suffering and Glory

[12]Beloved friends, if life gets extremely difficult, with many tests,[h] don't be bewildered as though something strange were overwhelming you.[i] [13]Instead,

---

a 4:7 Though the Greek uses only one word (sōphroneō), it is best defined by the two English words *intentional* and *purposeful.*

b 4:8 The Greek verb echō can also mean "to maintain, to possess, to keep, or to be so closely joined to something that you become its echo." In this case, we join ourselves so closely to God's love that we "echo" his forgiving, fervent love toward one another.

c 4:8 As translated from the Aramaic. See Proverbs 10:12 and 1 Corinthians 13:4–7.

d 4:9 As translated from the Aramaic and implied in the Greek, which can also be translated "Show hospitality to the stranger."

e 4:11 The Greek text is simply "If anyone speaks—as God's words." This would include preaching, teaching, and prophesying.

f 4:11 The Greek can also be translated "The one who provides finances should do it with the strength of God, who supplies all things."

g 4:11 Peter exhorts us in verses 7–11 to do five things as we see the end drawing closer: 1) be given to prayer, 2) be devoted to loving our fellow believers, 3) be compassionate to the stranger and foreigner, 4) use spiritual gifts to serve one another, 5) give God glory in all things.

h 4:12 Or "when the burning of a fiery trial is occurring among you."

i 4:12 The Aramaic adds a clause here: "because these things are your communion in the inheritance."

continue to rejoice, for you, in a measure, have shared in the sufferings of the Anointed One so that *you can share in* the revelation of his glory and celebrate with *even greater* gladness!*a* [14]If you are insulted because of the name of Christ, you are greatly blessed,*b* because the Spirit of glory and power,*c* who is the Spirit of God, rests upon you.*d*

[15]Let none of you merit suffering as a murderer, or thief, or criminal, or as one who meddles in the affairs of others. [16]If you suffer for being a Christian, don't consider it a disgrace but a *privilege*. Glorify God because you carry the Anointed One's name.*e* [17]For the time is ripe for judgment to begin in God's own household. And if it starts with us, what will be the fate of those who refuse to obey the gospel of God?

[18]And:

If the righteous are barely saved,*f*
what will become of the wicked and godless?*g*

[19]So then, those who suffer for following God's will should enfold their lives into the Creator, who will never fail them, and continue to always do what is right.*h*

---

a 4:13 The Greek verb tenses can imply either present or future. There is a glory unveiled in us as we focus on Christ in our difficulties. This brings immediate joy and rejoicing when we pass through suffering. Yet the greatest joy will be as we are free from mortal pain and see the revelation of his glory throughout eternity.

b 4:14 See Matthew 5:11.

c 4:14 Some Greek manuscripts have "and of power." The Aramaic reads, "the (Shekinah) glory of the Spirit."

d 4:14 See Isaiah 11:2. A few manuscripts, deemed unreliable, add, "On their part he is evil spoken of, but on your part he is glorified."

e 4:15 Or "that you bear this name." The word *Christian* means "anointed one." Christ is the Anointed One, and as his followers who are joined in life union to him, we too are "anointed ones."

f 4:18 The Aramaic is "if the righteous are harvested to salvation."

g 4:18 See Proverbs 11:31 LXX.

h 4:19 It is interesting that Peter points us to the Creator when we suffer. The faithful Creator, who keeps all things in order and feeds his creation, will never fail to be with us and supply grace and glory in all that we face.

Five

Elders and the Victor's Crown of Glory

[1]Now, I encourage you as an elder,[a] an eyewitness of the sufferings of Christ, and one who shares in the glory that is about to be unveiled. I urge my fellow elders among you [2]to be *compassionate* shepherds who *tenderly* care for God's flock and who feed them well, for you have the responsibility to guide, protect, and oversee. Consider it a joyous pleasure[b] and not merely a religious duty. Lead from the heart under God's leadership—not as a way to gain finances dishonestly but as a way *to* eagerly and cheerfully *serve*. [3]Don't be controlling tyrants[c] but lead others by your beautiful examples to the flock.[d] [4]And when the Shepherd-King[e] appears, you will win the victor's crown of glory that never fades away.[f]

[5]In the same way, the younger ones should willingly support[g] the leadership of the elders. In every relationship, each of you must wrap around yourself the apron of a humble servant. Because:

---

a 5:1 Peter had already identified himself as an apostle (1:1), but now he takes a humble position equal to that of local church elder. Peter's identification with the church elders becomes a powerful example of true spiritual leadership. The Aramaic uses the word *priest* instead of *elder*.

b 5:2 As translated from the Aramaic.

c 5:3 Or "masters of the flock (elevated above all others)."

d 5:3 As translated from the Aramaic.

e 5:4 Or "Chief Shepherd." The Aramaic is "Lord of the shepherds."

f 5:4 In these few verses Peter gives us the seven qualities of true shepherds who serve as elders for the flock: 1) They understand that they serve God's flock, not their own; 2) They lovingly guide and care for God's people; 3) They take the responsibilities of oversight willingly; 4) They are eager to serve, not eager for financial gain; 5) They feed and nurture God's people; 6) They reject a domineering leadership model; 7) They lead by examples of godliness and humility.

g 5:5 Although the Greek word *hupotasso* can be translated "submit," it is more often used for "support." See also Ephesians 5:21.

God resists you when you are proud
but multiplies grace and favor when you are humble.[a]

Humility and Faith

[6]If you bow low in God's awesome presence,[b] he will eventually exalt you as you leave the timing in his hands.

[7]Pour out all your worries and stress upon him *and leave them there*, for he always tenderly cares for you.[c]

[8]Be well balanced and always alert, because your enemy,[d] the devil, roams around incessantly, like a roaring lion looking for its prey to devour.[e] [9]Take a decisive stand against him and resist his every attack with strong, vigorous faith. For you know that your believing brothers and sisters around the world are experiencing the same kinds of troubles you endure.[f] [10]And then, after your brief suffering,[g] the God of all loving grace, who has called you to share in his eternal glory in Christ,[h] will personally and powerfully restore you and make you stronger than ever. Yes, he will set you firmly in

---

a 5:5 See Proverbs 3:34; James 4:6.

b 5:6 Or "under his mighty hands."

c 5:7 Or "Load upon him your every anxiety, for he is always watching over you with tender care." See also Psalm 55:22.

d 5:8 The Greek word *antidikos* is a legal term for one who presses a lawsuit that must be defended.

e 5:8 The implication in the context is that if you do not bring your worries and cares to God, the Devil will use depression and discouragement to devour you. Just as lions go after the feeble, the young, and the stragglers, so the enemy of our souls will always seek out those who are isolated, alone, or depressed to devour them.

f 5:9 Suffering, in part, comes from the activity of the Devil. There are sufferings that must be resisted in faith, as part of an attack from our adversary.

g 5:10 The Aramaic is "slight suffering." When we are in the midst of suffering, we are convinced it will never end. Peter reminds us that all of our trials are slight, brief, and temporary, but the glory we experience is eternal.

h 5:10 Some manuscripts have "Christ Jesus." The calling of every believer is to share in the glory of God unveiled in Christ. See John 17:22–24; Romans 8:18–21, 28–30; 2 Corinthians 4:17; 2 Timothy 2:10.

place and build you up.[a] [11]And he has all the power needed to do this[b]—forever![c] Amen.

Concluding Remarks

[12]I, Peter, with the help of Silas,[d] whom I consider a trustworthy, faith-filled brother, have written you this short letter so that I might encourage you and personally testify that this is the true, dependable grace of God.[e] Stand fast in this grace.

[13]She who is in Babylon,[f] who is co-elect with you, sends her greetings, along with Mark, my son.[g]

Greet one another with a kiss of peace.[h]

Peace to all who are in life union with Christ. Amen.

---

a 5:10 Peter knows what he is talking about. After his ordeal of denying three times that he even knew Jesus, God restored him and made him strong. Jesus prophesied to Peter that he would "strengthen the faith of [his] brothers." See Luke 22:31–32. Both of Peter's letters are anointed by the Holy Spirit to give you strong faith that will not give up.

b 5:11 Or "To him belongs all the power (to do this)."

c 5:11 Or "May power be to him forever!" That is, all the power needed to strengthen and build up God's people belongs to him.

d 5:12 Or "through Silvanus." This could mean that Silas (Silvanus) assisted Paul in writing this letter and/or that he was the courier who brought it to the churches. In the book of Acts, Silas was a ministry partner of Paul who accompanied him on his first and second missionary journeys (Acts 15:22) and was imprisoned with Paul in Philippi (Acts 16). However, in the epistles, Silas is named Silvanus (the Latin form of Silas). It is believed that Silas was one of the seventy disciples Jesus sent out and that he became the bishop of Thessalonica and was eventually martyred for his faith. The name Silas is the Greek form of the Aramaic name Saili (Saul).

e 5:12 The Aramaic adds a clause: "by which you have been resurrected."

f 5:13 Or "Your true sister in Babylon." This is a literal reference to the church of Babylon, according to the Aramaic. Since the Greek feminine pronoun is used here, many scholars have concluded that this is an allusion to the church, although some believe it could have been a reference to Peter's wife. Furthermore, Babylon may be a metaphor for the Roman Empire or even the city of Rome.

g 5:13 A possible reference to one of Peter's spiritual disciples, his "spiritual son" is most likely John Mark, a relative of Barnabas (Col. 4:10), who was the author of the gospel that bears his name. Many believe that Peter was the literary source for much of Mark's gospel. See also Acts 12:25–14:25; 15:36; 18:22; Philemon 24; 2 Timothy 4:11.

h 5:13 See also Romans 16:16; 1 Thessalonians 5:26.

2 Peter

TRIUMPHANT GRACE

Translator's Introduction to 2 Peter

AT A GLANCE

Author: The apostle Peter

Audience: Churches in Northwestern Asia Minor, modern Turkey

Date: AD 64–66

Type of Literature: A letter

Major Themes: God, humanity, salvation, ethics, eschatology, the church, and doctrine

Outline:
> Letter Opening — 1:1–11
> Peter's Reason for Writing — 1:12–15
> Issue 1: The Power and Appearing of Our Lord — 1:16–18
> Issue 2: The Reliable and Valid Prophetic Message — 1:19–21
> Issue 3: False Teachers and Their Sure Destruction — 2:1–22
> Issue 4: The Delay and Destruction of the Lord's Day — 3:1–13
> Letter Closing — 3:14–18

ABOUT 2 PETER

God has given us a treasure through the writings of the fisherman turned apostle, Simon Peter. With descriptive terms, this tremendous man writes a letter that will guard our souls through the revelation of God's triumphant grace. Not long before Peter was martyred he took up the quill to write to those who shared with him the glorious hope of eternal life. Read these three chapters to learn, to grow, and to be warned. We can accept all that he tells us, for it is the Word of God.

Peter, the one who was asked three times, "Does your heart burn with love for me," has filled his letter with multiple references to love. It is the perfect expression of the life of Christ within every believer. Love triumphs over troubles and pain. It perseveres in the truth when false teaching surrounds us. A fiery, endless love for Christ is the antidote to stagnancy in our spiritual lives. Peter will not let you forget the importance of this love, especially when it comes to your growth in Christ.

Spiritual growth is a process of learning to love, so Peter speaks about growing in God's triumphant grace and becoming fully mature as those who share the divine nature with Christ (1:4). It begins with faith and virtue but it ends with love. Our diligence to hold to our faith will be rewarded in time with a greater love for God and for his people.

And finally, Peter brings the return of Christ to prominence. He speaks of the end of time and what will happen. He points us to the sure word of prophecy, rising like a daystar in our hearts, affirming within us that Christ is coming back. Be prepared to find ample reasons in 2 Peter for your faith to grow, even if it means enduring hardships. We thank God for the words Peter has left us—words that will never fade away.

PURPOSE

Peter writes as one who is facing imminent death. He describes being an eyewitness to the transfiguration of Christ. The two major themes of 2 Peter that outline his purpose for writing could be described as *truth triumphant* and *love unending*. It is necessary to address false teaching wherever it may be found. But have no fear, truth will triumph every time—especially when we speak the truth in love.

The burden that motivated Peter to write this letter seems to be the multiple false teachings that were beginning to threaten the health of the churches. Apparently, the false teachers taught the people that our freedom in Christ meant that sexual immorality was not an issue that should trouble us (2:14). They even made a mockery of the second coming of Christ (3:3–4). How we need Peter's wise exhortation today to stay pure until the coming of the Lord! As such, one could view 2 Peter as his farewell letter to the churches he loved, urging them to stay the course until Christ's coming.

AUTHOR AND AUDIENCE

Although the authorship of 2 Peter is the most contested of all the New Testament books in our Bible, there should be no doubt that the beloved Peter the Rock is the human author of this inspired letter. In the third century Origen was the first of the church fathers to state that Peter was indeed the author, yet he did acknowledge that it was disputed by others. The stylistic differences are quite different between his first and second letter, but some scholars attribute this to a different amanuenses (secretary). Depending on the exact year Peter was martyred, we can approximate the date of writing this letter to AD 64–66.

It is believed that Peter was writing to churches within Northwest Asia Minor, which is modern-day Turkey. These communities included the Roman regions of Pontus, Galatia, Cappadocia, Asia, and Bithynia. Based on the content of the letter and purpose that drove Peter to write it, a number of false teachers had begun influencing them in a moral direction that ran contrary to their calling as God's children in Christ. Peter was concerned they were vulnerable to these teachers. So he wrote to them as a pastor, to stimulate them to wholesome, Christ-centered thinking, believing, and living.

MAJOR THEMES

God the Father, God the Son, God the Holy Spirit. Unlike 1 Peter, God the

Father is only mentioned a handful of times. Peter reveals he has created the cosmos and inspired the prophets; he is the ruler of angelic beings and human beings; the final judgment is described as "the coming day of God," yet he is also patient and merciful. However, where God the Father was prominent in letter one, in letter two he is more in the background.

Not true of God the Son! Jesus is clearly in the foreground in Peter's second letter, yet in a way that's unique: Jesus is most often mentioned with a corresponding descriptive expression. He is "our God and Savior" (1:1); he is "our Lord" (1:2); he is "our Lord and Savior," as well as "the Messiah" (1:10); and he is described as "the Master," our sovereign Lord (2:1). Additionally, except for 1:2, Peter refers to "Jesus Christ" or "Jesus the Messiah/ Anointed One" as one singular name. "Christ," "Messiah," "Anointed One" aren't merely titles for Jesus; it's who he is! He is the God-Savior, anointed by the Father, who reigns as supreme Lord.

Peter mentions the Holy Spirit only explicitly in 1:21, but he is also implied in 1:20. Though he occupies a small role in the letter, it isn't a minor one. For Peter's aim is to counter the false prophets affecting what these communities believed and how they lived. He wrote to remind the believers of their need to live a godly life and to confirm their calling. How are we to do that? We have "been given a prophetic message, reliable and fully validated" (1:19). And we can trust that message to guide our believing and behaving because those prophets were "inspired by the moving of the Holy Spirit" (1:21).

Entrapped Humanity and Divine Deliverance. Peter reveals something important about our human condition: humanity is entrapped by corrupt desires; God's goodness has opened a way to escape that corruption through deliverance. First, Peter makes known in his letter the reality that the world is filled with "corrupt desires." In fact, these desires are so powerful that they become entangled and defeated by them once again, to the point of losing the deliverance they'd gained and turning their backs against "the sacred obligation that was given to them" (2:21) in Christ.

And yet, Peter also makes known the revelation-truth that everything we need to "keep [us] from being inactive or fruitless in [our] pursuit of knowing Jesus Christ more intimately" and fully experiencing his deliverance has "already [been] planted deep within" (1:8). That's because through his divine initiative and by his divine power, God has called each of us by name and invited us to the rich experience of knowing Christ personally! For Peter, the idea of "knowing" is a crucial aspect of salvation. The Greek work *epignosis* carries with it the idea of acknowledging and recognizing Jesus as Lord and Savior, which leads to grace and peace, and the blossoming of Christian virtue.

Living in Light of the End. In 2 Peter, ethics (how we live) and eschatology (the end of the world) are intimately connected. In his final chapter, Peter draws our attention to the judgment that God will unfold on this reality, in preparation for a whole new one. But we aren't just waiting for the end; we're called to live in these "last days" in light of the end, the coming "day of God." Why? Because, as Peter reveals, in the end "every activity of man will be laid bare" (3:10). In light of this coming revelation and destruction he asks rhetorically, "Don't you see how vital it is to live a holy life?" Which is why "we must be consumed with godliness" (3:11), and why he urges his readers to "be eager to be found living pure lives when you come into his presence, without blemish, and filled with peace" (3:14).

False Teachers and False Teaching. One of the main reasons Peter wrote his letter was to urge the believing communities to guard against false teachers who would slip into their churches, secretly infiltrating them in order to divide and confuse them with destructive false teaching. Such people deny the sovereign Lord, live and teach immoral lifestyles, exploit true believers for their greedy gain, and pervert all kinds of Christian teachings and practices. While Peter does promise that "in their destruction they will be destroyed" (2:12), he also forewarns us not to be led astray by their lawlessness. Because for Peter, there is a very real threat of believers returning back to the very corrupt world system they escaped from in Christ! Peter believes right teachings are vital to the ongoing purity of the church and our individual godly lives.

$\mathcal{O}ne$

Introduction and Greeting

[1]*This letter is from* Simeon[a] Peter, a *loving* servant[b] and an apostle of Jesus Christ. I am writing to those who have been given a faith[c] as equally precious as ours through the righteousness of our God and Savior, Jesus Christ.[d] [2]May grace and perfect peace cascade over you[e] as you *live* in the rich knowledge of God and of Jesus our Lord.

God's Generous Grace

[3]Everything we could ever need for life and complete devotion[f] to God has already been deposited in us by his divine power. *For all this was lavished upon us* through the rich experience of knowing him who has called us by name and invited us to come to him through a glorious manifestation of his goodness.[g] [4]As a result of this, he has given you[h] magnificent promises[i] that

---

a 1:1 "Or "Simon," the Greek form of the Hebrew-Aramaic name Simeon. Simeon means "he who hears." Peter (the Rock) was the nickname given to him by Jesus; Simeon was his real name.

b 1:1 Or "bond-servant." From a Hebraic mind-set, this would imply a choice of remaining a servant even when freedom was offered. Thus, "a *loving* servant."

c 1:1 Even our faith has been given to us from a loving Father. Because our faith is equally precious as that of the apostles, we share an equal standing in the privileges and blessings of the kingdom realm of God.

d 1:1 In his opening verse, Peter points us to the deity of Jesus Christ—"God and Savior Jesus Christ" referring to one person. Some have described Peter's words to be the most clear and direct testimony to the truth of Christ's equality with God.

e 1:2 Or "May grace and peace be multiplied to you."

f 1:3 It is possible that this is a hendiadys, which would then mean "a life of godliness (complete devotion)." Everything we need to reflect God's true nature has already been given to us. See Ephesians 1:3.

g 1:3 Or "called us by his glory and goodness."

h 1:4 As translated from the Aramaic. The Greek is plural: *us*.

i 1:4 The Greek sentence that extends from verses 3–5 is somewhat ambiguous. It could also be read as "Through a glorious manifestation of his goodness he has imparted to us his magnificent promises."

are beyond all price, so that through *the power of* these tremendous promises[a] you can experience partnership[b] with the divine nature, by which you have escaped[c] the corrupt desires that are of the world.

Faith's Ladder of Virtue

[5] So devote yourselves[d] to lavishly supplementing[e] your faith with goodness,[f]
  and to goodness add understanding,
    [6] and to understanding add the strength of self-control,
  and to self-control add patient endurance,
  and to patient endurance add godliness,[g]
    [7] and to godliness add mercy toward your brothers and sisters,[h]
  and to mercy toward others add unending love.[i]

---

a 1:4 That is, by claiming these tremendous promises as our very own. Faith always releases the power of the Word of God.

b 1:4 The Greek word *koinonos* means "to participate as a partner, to partake of, to be a companion with, to have fellowship with" the divine nature. This is one of the great mysteries of our faith, that God shares his nature with us. We are given birth by the Holy Spirit to be God's true sons and daughters, and every father imparts his DNA and his "nature" to his children. The Greek word *physis* (nature) is taken from the word *phyō*, which means "to give birth, produce, bring forth, or to grow up." Christ lives in us and transforms us into his very own likeness. In Christ we share with him the divine nature. We will all bear the image of the Man from heaven, Jesus Christ. See Romans 8:9–25; 1 Corinthians 15:12–57.

c 1:4 The Greek word *apopheugō* also carries the connotation of being "acquitted."

d 1:5 Or "by having added your intense effort." The Aramaic is "by being under the weight of all these gifts."

e 1:5 The Greek word *epichorēgeo* means "to fully support the chorus" or "to completely choreograph."

f 1:5 Or "integrity, virtues of courage, nobleness, and moral valor."

g 1:6 Or "reverence."

h 1:7 As translated from the Aramaic and implied in the Greek. This mercy would include forgiveness and forbearance to those who fail.

i 1:7 It is possible to view this passage like an unfolding of faith: "Out of your faith will emerge goodness, and out of goodness will emerge understanding (of God), and out of understanding (of God) will emerge inner strength (self-control), and out of inner strength will emerge patient endurance, and out of patient endurance will emerge godliness, and out of godliness will emerge mercy toward your brothers and sisters, and out of mercy will emerge love." It is also possible to view this passage as a mathematical equation: faith + goodness = understanding. Goodness + understanding = inner strength.

⁸Since these virtues are already *planted* deep within,ᵃ and you possess them in abundant supply,ᵇ they will keep you from being inactive or fruitless in your pursuit of knowing Jesus Christ more intimately. ⁹But if anyone lacks these things, he is blind, constantly closing his eyes to the mysteries of our faith,ᶜ and forgetting *his innocence*—for his past sins have been washed away.ᵈ

¹⁰For this reason, beloved ones,ᵉ be eager to confirm and validateᶠ that God has invited you *to salvation*ᵍ and claimed youʰ as his own. If you do these things, you will never stumble. ¹¹As a result, the kingdom's gates will open wide to you as God choreographsⁱ your triumphant entrance into the eternal kingdom of our Lord and Savior, Jesus the Messiah.

Understanding + inner strength = patience. Inner strength + patience = godliness. Patience + godliness = mercy. And godliness + mercy = love.

a 1:8 The Greek word *hyparchō* means to "begin below (or within, like a plant growing beneath the ground)."

b 1:8 Or "abounding (repeatedly being more than enough)."

c 1:9 Although the Greek word *myōpazō* can mean "nearsighted," it is a compound word taken from the base word *mystērion* (mystery), and *optonomai* (to look upon, to behold). The implication is that when the virtues of the divine nature are not flourishing in believers, it is because they are *closing their eyes* to the mysteries of our faith; i.e., Christ in us, the hope of glory. See Colossians 1:27.

d 1:9 The Aramaic can be translated "He is still searching for the purification of his original sins."

e 1:10 Or "brothers (and sisters)."

f 1:10 The Aramaic adds the phrase "by your good deeds." The implication is that by developing the virtues Peter has spoken of in verses 3–7, we validate God's calling and choice of us.

g 1:10 We have a confident assurance that we have been chosen and called to salvation by God himself. This is a firm foundation on which to build our lives. We can grow in that confidence as we see the work of the Spirit bearing spiritual fruit through our lives. See Galatians 5:22–23; 2 Timothy 2:19; 1 John 3:10, 14. The Greek for "invited you" is *klēsis*, which means "to invite (summon) to a feast."

h 1:10 The Greek word for "claimed as his own" is *eklogē* (from his *logos* word). God spoke and you were his. You are meant to be a "chosen word" from his mouth, and you will not return to him void, but you will accomplish what he has destined for you to do.

i 1:11 This is the Greek word *epichorēgeo*, which can mean "richly provide (for the choir)" or "choreograph." The Lord of the dance will richly welcome you into his eternal kingdom. See Zephaniah 3:17.

Divine Revelation

[12]I won't hesitate to continually remind you of these truths, even though you are aware of them and are well established in the present measure of truth you have already embraced.[a] [13]And as long as I live[b] I will continue to awaken you with this reminder, [14]since our Lord Jesus, the Anointed One, has clearly revealed that my departure is near.[c] [15]Indeed, I'm passionate[d] to share these things with you so that you will always remember them after my exodus from this life.

Jesus' Transfiguration

[16]We were not retelling some masterfully crafted legend when we informed you of the power and appearing of our Lord Jesus Christ,[e] for we saw his magnificence and splendor *unveiled* before our very eyes.[f] [17]Yes, Father God lavished upon him radiant glory and honor when his distinct voice spoke out of the realm of majestic glory,[g] endorsing him with these words: **This is my cherished Son, marked by my love. All my delight is found in him!**[h] [18]And we ourselves heard that voice resound from the heavens while we were with him on the holy mountain.

---

a 1:12 Or "in the measure of truth that has reached you." The implication is that there is yet more truth for every follower of Jesus to learn and embrace.

b 1:13 Or "as long as I am in this tent."

c 1:14 Or "that the removal of my tent is soon," a euphemism for Peter's death. See John 21:18–19. The apostle Peter knew that death was coming soon for him. Indeed, in AD 68 he was crucified upside down in Rome, at his own request, so as not to die in the same manner as Jesus.

d 1:15 Or "make every effort."

e 1:16 A possible hendiadys, "the powerful coming of our Lord Jesus Christ in power" or "the appearing of our powerful Lord Jesus Christ." The Aramaic is "the power and comingness of our Master, Jesus Christ."

f 1:16 See Matthew 17:1–8; Mark 9:1–7; Luke 9:27–36.

g 1:16 A possible periphrastic reference to God, "the Transcendent Glory."

h 1:17 Or "On him my favor rests." The Aramaic is "in whom I am fulfilled."

Prophecy

[19]And so we have been given the prophetic word—the *written*[a] message of the prophets, made more reliable and fully validated *by the confirming voice of God on the Mount of Transfiguration.*[b] And you will continue to do well if you stay focused on it. *For this prophetic message* is like a piercing light[c]

---

a 1:19 The phrase *prophetic word*, or "word of prophecy," when found in Christian writing through the second century, is used only for Old Testament Scriptures. See Peter Davids, *The Letters of 2 Peter and Jude* (Grand Rapids, MI: Eerdmans, 2006), 207; Gene Green, *Jude and 2 Peter* (Grand Rapids, MI: Baker Academic, 2008), 227; David Walls and Max Anders, *The Holman New Testament Commentary: 1 and 2 Peter; 1, 2 and 3 John and Jude* (Nashville, TN: B&H Publishing, 1999), 113. See also Luke 24:25; John 6:45; Isaiah 8:20.

b 1:19 The comparative adjective bebaioteron (more reliable) serves as a predicate adjective. "And we have the prophetic word as more certain," meaning that the transfiguration confirmed (made more certain) the witness of the OT Scriptures to Jesus as Messiah, the Son of God, who brought his eternal kingdom on earth (2 Peter 1:11). The witness of God's Spirit through the transfiguration complements the witness of the OT Scriptures in 2 Peter 1:19—both confirm that Jesus is the Messiah, God's Son, who will return to rule on earth. See Peter Davids, *The Letters of 2 Peter and Jude* (Grand Rapids, MI: Eerdmans, 2006), 207. What is said to be made more certain or reliable is "the word of the prophets." This has bothered some commentators in that it places experience ahead of the prophetic word, so they argue that the prophetic word makes the transfiguration more certain, citing later Jewish opinion that even a voice (*bat qol*) from heaven could not overrule a Scripture. That, however, is not what the grammar of the text indicates. Instead, we see that "the word of the prophets" is what is made more certain/reliable. See also: M. Zerwick and M. Grosvenor, *A Grammatical Analysis of the Greek New Testament*, 3rd rev. edition (Rome: Editrice Pontificio Istituto Biblico, 1988), 719; Lewis R. Donelson, *1 and 2 Peter and Jude* (Louisville, KY: Westminster John Knox, 2010), 234: "This means that the account of the transfiguration makes OT prophecy more reliable. . . . The giving of honor and glory to Jesus at the transfiguration reinforces the credibility of OT prophecies about the messiah"; D. P. Senior and D. J. Harrington, 1 Peter, Jude and 2 Peter (Collegeville, MN: Liturgical Press, 2008), 257: "The idea seems to be that the transfiguration and all that pertains to Jesus fulfills and thus confirms what the prophets said and so makes them even 'all the more reliable'"; the same view was also held by the well-known Greek scholar of the early twentieth century; A. T. Robertson, *Word Pictures of the New Testament*, vol. 6 (Nashville, TN: Broadman Press, 1931), p. 157.

c 1:19 Or "lamp." See Psalm 119:105.

shining in a gloomy place[a] until the dawning of a new day,[b] when the Morning Star[c] rises in your hearts.[d]

[20]You must understand this at the outset: Interpretation of scriptural prophecy *requires the Holy Spirit,* for it does not originate from someone's own imagination.[e] [21]No true prophecy comes from human initiative but is inspired by the moving of the Holy Spirit upon those[f] who spoke the message that came from God.[g]

Two

Warning about False Teachers

[1]In the past there arose false prophets[h] among *God's* people, just as there will continue to be false teachers who will secretly infiltrate in your midst *to divide*

---

a 1:19 This dismal or dark/murky place can be both the world in which we live and the human heart bathed in the light of truth, displacing gloom and darkness. See Isaiah 9:1.

b 1:19 See Luke 1:78.

c 1:19 Or "Light Bearer." The Aramaic is "until the sun rises in your hearts." See Revelation 22:16.

d 1:19 This is not simply a far-off future event of Christ's coming but the internal promise of his light and power subduing our hearts, as Christ rises within us like the dawning of the new day and like the morning star. The dawn conquers the night, and the morning star promises the new day appearing.

e 1:20 The Greek text is somewhat ambiguous and can be translated in three ways: 1) No prophecy can be interpreted by the prophet's own imagination; that is, they didn't make things up. 2) No prophecy can be interpreted by itself, for other Scriptures are needed to understand and interpret biblical prophecy. 3) No prophecy can be interpreted by one's own imagination, for the help of the Holy Spirit, who inspired it, is needed to interpret it. The Aramaic is "No prophecy is ever fulfilled as soon as it is written."

f 1:21 Some Greek manuscripts have "holy men (and women)."

g 1:21 This is a clear reference to the doctrine of the inspiration of the Scriptures. It is God's words spoken (prophecy) and written, as given by the Holy Spirit. God speaks through people his inspired and trustworthy words. See also 2 Timothy 3:16–17.

h 2:1 Or "Pretend prophets birthed themselves."

you, bringing with them their destructive heresies.[a] They will even deny the Master, who paid the price for them, bringing swift destruction on themselves. ²Many will follow immoral lifestyles.[b] Because of these *corrupt false teachers*, the way of truth[c] will be slandered. ³They are only out for themselves,[d] ready to exploit you for their own gain through their cunning arguments. Their condemnation has been a long time coming. But their destruction does not slumber[e] or sit idly by, *for it is sure to come*.

⁴Now, *don't forget*, God had no pity for the angels when they sinned[f] but threw them into the lowest, darkest dungeon of gloom[g] and locked them in chains, where they are firmly held until the judgment of torment.[h]

⁵And he did not spare the former world[i] *in the days of Noah* when he sent a flood to destroy a depraved world[j] (although he protected Noah, the preacher of righteousness, along with seven members of his family).[k]

⁶And *don't forget that* he reduced to ashes the cities of Sodom and Gomorrah, condemning them to ruin and destruction.[l] God appointed them to be examples as to what is coming to the ungodly.[m] ⁷Yet he rescued

---

a 2:1 Or "destructive ways of thinking (viewpoints)."

b 2:2 Or "sensualities (outrageous behaviors)."

c 2:2 Or "the true Way." Some manuscripts have "the glory of the truth."

d 2:3 Or "With greed."

e 2:3 The Aramaic is "Abaddon never slumbers." *Abaddon* is a Hebrew term for the realm of the dead and symbolizes the bottomless pit.

f 2:4 Because of the context of Noah's flood, these were possibly the "Watchers," angels who sinned and rebelled against God's laws by having sexual relations with women, thus producing offspring (Gen. 6:1–4). They are mentioned in Daniel 4:13, 17, 23; Jude 6–7; the Book of 1 Enoch 6–10; the Book of Jubilees 5; and the Dead Sea scrolls (The Book of Giants). God put them in chains (ropes) and bound them in Tartarus (the deepest pit of gloom) until their final judgment.

g 2:4 The Greek uses the term Tartarus, a Hellenistic mythical term for the subterranean underworld, the lowest pit (of hell).

h 2:4 As translated from the Aramaic and two older Greek uncials.

i 2:5 Or "original world."

j 2:5 Or "a world devoid of awe."

k 2:5 See Genesis 6–8 and 1 Peter 3:20.

l 2:6 See Genesis 19.

m 2:6 Or "as an example to the ungodly of coming generations." After seeing these three examples (fallen angels, people who lived at the time of the flood, Sodom and Gomora righteous man, Lot, suffering the indignity of the unbridled lusts of the lawless.[a] [8]For righteous Lot lived among them day after day, distressed in his righteous soul by the rebellious deeds he saw and heard.

[9]If the Lord Yahweh *rescued Lot,* he knows how to continually rescue the godly from their trials and to reserve the ungodly for punishment on the day of judgment.[b] [10]And this especially applies to those who live their lives despising authorities[c] and who abandon themselves to chasing the depraved lusts of their flesh.

The Arrogance of False Teachers

They are willfully arrogant and insolent, unafraid to insult the glorious ones.[d] [11]Yet even angels, who are greater than they in power and strength, do not dare slander them before the Lord.[e] [12]These individuals are nothing but brute beasts—irrational creatures, born in the wild to be caught and destroyed—and they will perish like beasts. They are professional insulters, who slander whatever they don't understand, and in their destruction they will be destroyed. [13]For all the evil they have done will come crashing down on them. They consider it their great pleasure to carouse in broad daylight. When they come to your love feasts[f] they are but stains and blemishes, reveling in their deceptions as they feast with you. [14]They are addicted to adultery, with eyes

---

rah), it is difficult to believe that everyone will ultimately be saved. There is a doom that awaits the ungodly (those who do not believe in Jesus Christ, the Savior).

a 2:7 As translated from the Aramaic.

b 2:9 Or "to keep the unrighteous under punishment until the day of judgment," which implies that the wicked are living under God's punishment even before they are ultimately judged.

c 2:10 Or "despising realms of power (authority)." The Aramaic is "They do not tremble with awe while they blaspheme."

d 2:10 Or "slandering reputations" or "blaspheming glories (dignitaries)." Because of the context, most believe this is speaking of *glorious* celestial beings in heaven (e.g., archangels). See Jude 8–10.

e 2:11 Some manuscripts do not have "before the Lord."

f 2:13 Peter equates the gatherings of believers as "love feasts." Our true purpose in coming together is to magnify and feast on the love of Christ, sharing his love with all.

that are insatiable,[a] with sins that never end. They seduce the vulnerable and are experts in their greed—they are but children of a curse!

The Example of Balaam

[15]They have wandered off the main road and have gone astray, because they are prophets who love profit—the wages they earn by wrongdoing. They are following the example of Balaam, son of Beor,[b] [16]who was rebuked for evil by a donkey incapable of speech yet that spoke with a human voice and restrained the prophet's madness.[c]

[17]These people are dried-up riverbeds, waterless clouds pushed along by stormy winds—the deepest darkness of gloom has been prepared for them. [18]They spout off with their grandiose, impressive nonsense. Consumed with the lusts of the flesh, they lure *back into sin* those who recently escaped from their error. [19]They promise others freedom, yet they themselves are slaves to corruption, for people are slaves to whatever overcomes them.

[20]Those who escape the corrupting forces of this world system through the experience of knowing about our Lord and Savior, Jesus the Messiah, then go back into entanglement with them and is defeated by them, become worse off than they were to start with. [21]It would have been much better for them never to have experienced the way of righteousness than to know it and then turn away from the sacred obligation[d] that was given to them. [22]They become illustrations of the true proverb:

A dog will return to his own vomit[e]
and a washed pig to its rolling in the mud.

---

a 2:14 Or "Their eyes are full of an adulteress."

b 1:15 Or "Bosor."

c 2:16 See Numbers 22–24.

d 2:21 Or "holy command."

e 2:22 See Proverbs 26:11. The rest of the proverb is believed to be a quote from Heraclitus of Ephesus, known as the "weeping philosopher" (535–475 BC).

Three

The Coming of the Lord

[1]Beloved friends, this is now the second letter I have written to you[a] in which I've attempted to stir you up and awaken you to a proper mind-set.[b] [2]So never forget both the prophecies spoken by the holy prophets of old and the teaching[c] of our Lord and Savior spoken by your apostles.[d]

[3]Above all, you must understand that in the last days mockers[e] will multiply, chasing after their evil desires. [4]They will say, "So what about this promise of his coming?[f] Our ancestors are dead and buried, yet everything is still the same as it was since from the beginning of time until now. "

[5]But they conveniently overlook that from the beginning, the heavens and earth were created by God's word. *He spoke* and the dry ground separated from the waters. [6]Then long afterward he destroyed the world with a tremendous flood by those very waters.[g] [7]And now, by the same *powerful* word, the heavens and the earth are reserved for fire,[h] being kept for judgment day, when all the ungodly will perish.

[8]So, dear friends, don't let this one thing escape your notice: a single

---

a 3:1 This would indicate that Peter is writing to the same people as his first letter (Galatia, Cappadocia, and the Roman province of Asia).

b 3:1 Or "a pure mind" or "sincere intention." The Aramaic is "Awaken your beautiful memories."

c 3:2 Or "commandment."

d 3:2 Peter places "your apostles" on the same level as the Old Testament prophets as to their trustworthiness and in setting the standard for living a life of purity for God.

e 3:3 Or "deceivers."

f 3:4 This is the Greek word *Parousia,* which can also mean "presence" or "arrival" or "visitation." The Aramaic is "Where is the kingdom that he brought?"

g 3:6 Verses 5–6 are translated from the Aramaic. The Greek could be translated "The word of the Lord formed the heavens and the earth out of water and by means of water. And it was destroyed by the submerging of the world of that day—destroyed by water."

h 3:7 The Aramaic is "The earth is being kept as a hayloft (or pile of hay) for the fire."

2 PETER THREE • 43

day counts like a thousand years to the Lord Yahweh,[a] and a thousand years counts as one day.[b] [9]This means that, *contrary to man's perspective,* the Lord is not late with his promise *to return,* as some measure lateness. But rather, his "delay" simply reveals his loving patience toward you, because he does not want any to perish but all to come to repentance.[c]

[10]The day of the Lord will come and take everyone by surprise—as unexpected as a home invasion. The atmosphere will be set on fire and vanish with a horrific roar, and the heavenly bodies[d] will melt away as in a tremendous blaze. The earth and every activity of man will be laid bare.[e] [11]Since all these things are on the verge of being dismantled, don't you see how vital it is to live a holy life? We must be consumed with godliness [12]while we anticipate and help to speed up[f] the coming of the day of God, when the atmosphere will be set on fire and the heavenly bodies consumed in a blaze. [13]But as we wait, we trust in God's royal proclamation to be fulfilled. There are coming[g] heavens new in quality, and an earth new in quality, where righteousness will be fully at home.[h]

---

a 3:8 As translated from the Aramaic.

b 3:8 Peter gives us an incredible interpretive key to understand time from the Lord's perspective. A day and a thousand years can both be symbolic. See also Psalm 90:4.

c 3:9 The Aramaic is quite different and can be translated "The Lord does not treat his kingdom like a dutiful chore, as some people consider it, like the treatment of a temporary laborer. But he pours out his Spirit on your behalf, since he does not wish that anyone should perish but that everyone should come into grace."

d 3:10 Or "elements."

e 3:10 The Aramaic can be translated "The earth and its works will be refined."

f 3:12 Peter is teaching us that the church has the ability to speed up (and, by implication, slow down) the coming of the day of God. The closer we get to Christ, the closer will be his coming. *The day of God* is an equivalent phrase to the "day of the Lord."

g 3:13 As translated from the Aramaic. The Aramaic word for promise is best translated "royal proclamation."

h 3:13 See Isaiah 65:17 and 66:22. There is coming a day when all will live according to God's perfect will for their lives and righteousness will be at home on earth and in every heart. This will be the day when justice reigns on earth. The Aramaic is "We expect from his promise a new sky and a new earth in which the virtuous people will dwell."

Preparation for the Coming of the Lord

[14]So, my beloved friends, with all that you have to look forward to, may you be eager to be found living pure lives when you come into his presence,[a] without blemish and filled with peace. [15]And keep in mind that our Lord's extraordinary patience simply means *more opportunity for* salvation,[b] just as our dear brother Paul wrote to you with the wisdom that God gave him. [16]He consistently speaks of these things in all of his letters, even though he writes some concepts that are overwhelming to our understanding, which the unlearned and unstable love to twist to their *spiritual* ruin, as they do to other Scriptures.[c]

Grow in God's Grace

[17]As for you, divinely loved ones, since you are forewarned of these things, be careful that you are not led astray by the error of the lawless and lose your firm grip *on the truth.* [18]But continue to grow and increase in God's grace and intimacy with our Lord and Savior, Jesus Christ.[d] May he receive all the glory both now and until the day eternity begins. Amen!

---

a 3:14 Although this is clearly implied, it is based on the dative pronoun *autō,* which does not indicate agency (by him), but in his presence (before him).

b 3:15 See 2 Peter 3:9. The Aramaic is "Consider the Lord's outpouring of (his) Spirit as salvation."

c 3:16 This is not meant to imply that we cannot understand the Bible, but that there are certain concepts that are difficult to understand. The Bible is the only book whose Author is present every time it is read. The Holy One is the Divine Author of Scripture (2 Timothy 3:16) and is the one who can open our hearts to understand truth. It is when we twist the Scriptures to fit our understanding that we are distorting its truth. Note also that Peter places Paul's letters in the same category as the "other (inspired) Scriptures."

d 3:18 The Aramaic does not use the imperative but makes it more of a decree: "You continue to be nourished in grace and in the intimate knowledge of our Lord and Savior, Jesus the Messiah, and of God the Father." Spiritual growth is yielding to the grace of God and having passion to know Jesus Christ intimately. In time, we grow into his beautiful image.

GOD IS LOVE

Translator's Introduction to 1 John

AT A GLANCE

Author: The apostle John

Audience: Communities in Asia Minor experiencing schism

Date: AD 85

Type of Literature: A letter

Major Themes: Preserving truth, false teaching, God's character, Christ's centrality, and Christian discipleship

Outline:
Letter Opening —1:1–4
Walk in God's Light, Keep God's Commands —1:5–2:11
New Status, New Love —2:12–17
Believing and Living as God's Children — 2:18–3:24
Test the Spirits — 4:1–6
Love for Another, Love for God — 4:7–5:12
Letter Closing — 5:13–21

ABOUT 1 JOHN

God is love! Let these words live within you! The glorious God of love is revealed in John's three letters. Written by the same John who penned his gospel, the reader is taken into the Light of God. These beautiful words should be read over and over by every person on earth. God is love, and you can come to him by faith!

Everyone needs assurance from God that they are loved and cherished. The apostle John wrote this letter to assure us of the truths of God's love and mercy toward us. And when we receive his love, we are free to share it with others. As we love one another, we have the assurance that we are God's true spiritual children and God's love is perfected in us. What joy John's words bring to our hearts!

Although the author is not named, it was clearly John the Beloved[a] who wrote this letter. He once walked on the shore of the Lake of Galilee—a fisherman, who left all to follow Jesus. And he taught all about life—eternal life, glorious life, abundant life! In Christ we find life, so John will always point us to Christ and our fellowship with him. In fact, John tells us four reasons why he wrote his letters:

1) To bring us into life-union (fellowship) with God (1 John 1:3).
2) That we might experience the fullness of joy (1 John 1:4).
3) That we might not sin (1 John 2:1).
4) That we might have the full assurance of our salvation (1 John 5:13).

The beloved apostle of Jesus reveals to us the revelation knowledge of who Jesus is and who we have become in him. John is the apostle of love. This letter is saturated with the love of God, which has been lavished upon us in Christ. And this love must be seen, made visible as we express his love toward one another. John reinforces this truth: we are to be ministers of love in how we walk in this life, demonstrating truth and kindness to all.

---

a Only the New Testament books of Hebrews and 1 John do not directly name its author.

John's letter will bring a fresh understanding of God to your heart. Let him speak to you through his faithful servant John. Enjoy!

PURPOSE

John the beloved wrote his magisterial letter to bring the church back into unity and clarity of faith, and beckon her to hold fast to the tradition and values they had already committed themselves to in Christ. There were false teachers who had come in and divided the flock with doctrines that diminished the glory of Christ. John's teachings always take us deeper into the truth and ways of God, and deeper into love for Jesus Christ. Anything that moves the heart away from loving Christ and loving others is to be viewed as suspect and diversionary. We can thank God for John's three letters to consistently point us back to the Light!

AUTHOR AND AUDIENCE

Although some contest it, there should be little doubt that the apostle John was responsible for writing this letter of passion, probably while he was in Ephesus around AD 85. The opening of the letter itself bears striking similarity to the gospel that bears his name, extolling the Living Expression of God in almost poetic language. There are at least twelve other passages that have direct connection in both language, style, and scope with the fourth gospel—showing that the beloved disciple of Jesus was the author of this beloved letter.

Unlike his other two letters, 1 John is not addressed to certain ones but to everyone. No particular audience is addressed in this letter, although there was a community over which John was an overseer in spiritual authority and fatherhood. Many believe John wrote this letter to clarify what he wrote earlier about the truth of Christ and to correct misinterpretations and misapplication of his testimony, especially by false teachers who had infiltrated this community. It was meant to encourage the believers who had been scattered by the Roman War of AD 67–70, and serve to encourage them in their understanding of their faith.

MAJOR THEMES

Preserving and Discerning Truth. In John's first gospel, he wrote his account of Jesus' life "so that you will fully believe that Jesus is the Anointed One, the Son of God" (20:31). He testified to the same truth in this letter so that those who believed wouldn't be led astray and would be "assured and know without a doubt that you have eternal life." Such assurance and knowledge comes through the truth about Jesus, the Anointed One and Son of God, which John sought to preserve and help believers discern.

John was writing to a community by false teachers who had distorted the truth of the gospel. For John, *truth* and *gospel* are equated, for the good news is about the one who was the Truth. So he defined a number of truths that one must believe in order to know eternal life, and encouraged ongoing discernment of the truth. Discernment is a major theme in this letter, and it is the task of the church to test the spirits, to "carefully examine what they say to determine if they are of God" (4:1).

Warning Against Antichrists. John warns us that we must set our hearts firmly on the truths of Jesus Christ and his word as protection from those whom John called *antichrists.* These people opposed the teachings of Christ, led people astray, and separated from the true community of Christ followers. John refuted antichrists in his day in a number of ways: he appealed to the teachings that had been with the church from the beginning; referenced early confessed creeds; pointed to the teachings and example of Jesus; appealed to the guidance of the Holy Spirit for all truth; and referenced our personal experience with God's heart through salvation. We guard against false teachers in these last days when we heed John's warnings and follow his guidance.

The Character of God. One of the more profound unveilings in 1 John is the character of God. Take a look at all we learn about him in John's Spirit-anointed letter: God is pure light, without a trace of darkness or impurity; faithfully forgives us of our sins, cleansing us from all unrighteousness; the essence of love, for he continually exists being love; the reality of all that is true; and the Father God who saves, having sent his Son into the world as its Savior. Ultimately, everything that is true about God is ours, because we have been born of God and enjoy unbroken fellowship with him.

The Centrality of Christ. It's only when we properly understand who Jesus Christ is that we can experience the heart of God. A distorted picture of Christ distorts how we live, which is why Christ takes center stage in John's letter. Every chapter is fixed on him: he is unveiled as the Living Expression of God; he is our atoning sacrifice, the one who shed his blood for our sins; he is our *paraclete* who advocates before the Father's throne on our behalf; he is our standard for living, the one in whom we are to actively remain; he will transform us into himself when he appears; he has come in real life flesh, not merely as a spirit-presence; and our new birth depends on believing in him, for he is the center of our believing as much as our faith.

Walking as Disciples of Christ. John's letter is largely concerned with preserving and discerning the truth about Jesus. Yet truth isn't only something to know in the head; it's something that we do with our whole self. John uses the metaphor of "walking" for the kind of life we're called to live—an image from the Hebrew Scriptures suggesting a manner and style of living that one is fully committed to. We are to walk in the pure light, not the realm of darkness; we are to walk in self-sacrificing love, not hate. Disciples of Christ walk the truth, which manifests itself as love. Of course, we know what love is because of Jesus: "This is how we have discovered love's reality: Jesus sacrificed his life for us!" (3:16). John says the essence of our Christian life is emulating this love, which results in fellowship with God.

One

The Living Expression

[1]We saw him with our very own eyes.[a]
We gazed upon him[b] and heard him speak.[c]
Our hands actually touched him,[d]
the one who was from the beginning,
the Living Expression of God.[e]
[2]This Life-Giver was made visible
and we have seen him.
We testify to this truth:
the eternal Life-Giver
lived face-to-face with the Father
and has now dawned upon us.
[3]So we proclaim to you
what we have seen and heard
about this Life-Giver
so that we may share and enjoy

---

a 1:1 Or "We perceived (experienced) him with our eyes."

b 1:1 The apostles gazed upon Jesus both during Christ's earthly life and in resurrection glory.

c 1:1 The Aramaic text yields an interesting thought. By using the words *one* and *heard* in the same context, we're taken back to the ancient prayer of the Hebrews known as the Shema: "*Hear,* O Israel, the Lord our God is *one.*" John is stating that he has heard the one that Israel was commanded to listen to, and that "one" is Jesus Christ. See Deuteronomy 6:4.

d 1:1 The word for touch is poetic. It comes from a sensory verb meaning "to pluck the strings of an instrument." It can also be translated "to feel" (see Acts 17:27). It is as though John is saying, "We have plucked the chords of his being and felt what motivated him, his melody within."

e 1:1 Or "Word (Logos) of life." See footnote on John 1:1. This verse in both Greek and Aramaic breaks many rules of grammar and is used as a poetic tool to pack deep revelation in as few words as possible.

this life together.
For truly our fellowship[a] is with the Father
and with his Son, Jesus, the Anointed One.[b]

⁴We are writing these things to you because we want to release to you our fullness of joy.[c]

God Is Light

⁵This is the life-giving message[d] we heard him share *and it's still ringing in our ears*. We now repeat his words to you: **God is pure light. You will never find even a trace of darkness in him.**[e]

⁶If we claim that we share life with him,[f] but keep walking in the realm of darkness, we're fooling ourselves and not living the truth. ⁷But if we keep living in the pure light that surrounds him,[g] we share *unbroken* fellowship

---

a 1:3 The Greek word *koinōnia* means "to share in partnership; a reality shared in common." Through Christ, our shared reality is now with the Father. See also 2 Peter 1:4.

b 1:3 It is believed that these first three verses comprised an early hymn sung by the church.

c 1:4 Or "that our joy may be fulfilled." The first four verses form one Greek sentence, somewhat awkward in its construction, with three parenthetical interruptions in the sequence of the Greek sentence, which would be confusing if left in a literal form. This translation attempts to make one long, complicated Greek sentence into a meaningful translation of what John wrote.

d 1:5 The Greek word for "life-giving message (promise)" is *angelia* and is found only twice in the New Testament. It is related semantically to *euangelion,* which means "to evangelize or preach the (life-giving) gospel." The Aramaic is "This is the hope that we heard from him and give you hope because God is light and there is absolutely no darkness in him."

e 1:5 Or "No darkness at all can find any place in him." Although we do not have these exact words in any of the four Gospels, it is clear that John and the apostles attributed these words to Jesus Christ. Not everything Jesus said or did is recorded in the Gospels. If all of the events given in Matthew, Mark, Luke, and John were condensed, we would only have details recorded of but a few months of Jesus' entire life of over thirty-three years. See John 21:25.

f 1:6 Or "We share in fellowship with him (Gr. *koinōnia,* "having things in common; sharing in what he has and who he is")." This is the first of six conditional "if" clauses that extend through 2:1.

g 1:7 Or "as he (Christ) is in the light."

with one another,[a] and the blood of Jesus, his Son, continually cleanses us from all sin.

Purified from Sin

[8]If we boast that we have no sin, we're only fooling ourselves and are strangers to the truth. [9]But if we freely admit our sins *when his light uncovers them*,[b] he will be faithful to forgive us every time. God is just to forgive us our sins *because of Christ*, and he will continue to cleanse us from all unrighteousness.[c]

[10]If we claim that we're not guilty of sin *when God uncovers it with his light*,[d] we make him a liar and his word is not in us.

---

a 1:7 That is, God and the believer enjoy fellowship on the basis of walking in the light of God. Fellowship is maintained with God as we continue walking in the light he reveals to us. To walk in the light also involves being open, transparent, and honest, acknowledging any darkness the Lord might reveal in us. The blood of Jesus will cleanse us from all known sin, and if we continue to be open to God's pure light, his blood will cleanse us from all unknown sin as well, enabling imperfect believers to walk in fellowship with a holy God. Freedom from sin (which is mentioned seventeen times in 1 John) is equated to walking in the pure light of God—not simply a fleshly struggle but a desire to walk in fellowship with God in his light.

b 1:9 Confession of sin is the way to find restoration and unbroken fellowship with God. It cleanses the conscience and removes every obstacle from communion with Christ. Confession does not gain God's acceptance, for that was won for us forever by the sacrifice of Christ. It is on the basis of being his dearly loved children that we restore intimacy with God through our tenderhearted confession before him. God will always be faithful to restore our first-love passion for him. There is no need to confess the same sins over and over, for that is ignoring the blood of Jesus that cleanses us. All of our sins were paid for on the cross and we can do nothing to remove them, but confession acknowledges God's faithfulness to restore our intimacy with him. Our Father and our forgiving Redeemer fill the heavens with grace toward every believer, even when we sin.

c 1:9 Unrighteousness, in this context, means the sins we're not aware of. Confession cleanses known sin and restores fellowship with God, but God's faithfulness, in seeing Christ as our Sin-Bearer, cleanses us from all unknown sin as well. If we do but one thing (confess our sin), God will do four things: 1) demonstrate his faithful love, 2) demonstrate justice by counting our sins paid for by Christ, 3) forgive us every sin, and 4) continue a deeper work of cleansing from all aspects of sin's defilement.

d 1:10 We can only confess what God has revealed to us in his light. But when he shows that a thought or life pattern is sinful, we must agree with him in order to be restored. We cannot hide or conceal our sin, but confess our failure to him and move forward in faith. This is like a "rebound" for a missed shot.

Two

Christ, Our Answer for Sin

[1] You are my dear children, and I write these things to you so that you won't sin. But if anyone does sin, we continually have a forgiving Redeemer[a] who is face-to-face with the Father:[b] Jesus Christ, the Righteous One. [2] He is the atoning sacrifice[c] for our sins, and not only for ours but also for the sins of the whole world.[d]

The New Commandment

[3] Here's how we can be sure that we've truly come to know God: if we keep his commands.[e] [4] If someone claims, "I have come to know God *by experience*," yet doesn't keep God's commands, he is a phony and the truth finds no place in him. [5] But whoever keeps God's words will experience the mature love of God has reached perfection within him.

We can be sure that we've truly come to live in *intimacy with God*, [6] not just by saying, "I am intimate with God," but by walking in the footsteps of Jesus.

[7] Beloved, I'm not writing a new commandment to you, but an old one that you had from the beginning, and you've already heard it.[f] [8] Yet, in a sense, it is a new commandment,[g] as its truth is made manifest both in Christ

---

a 2:1 Or "Advocate." The Aramaic is "the Redeemer who ends the curse." See John 14:16 and accompanying footnote.

b 2:1 Or "who is face-to-face with the Father." He is still our Father even when we sin.

c 2:2 Or "satisfaction for our sins" or "atoning sacrifice for our sins."

d 2:2 In these two verses we find three things that Christ is to us: 1) our forgiving Redeemer/Intercessor, 2) the Righteous One who suffered in our place, 3) the atoning sacrifice for our sins, which cleanses and shelters us.

e 2:3 Keeping God's commands is the proof and evidence of coming to know God, not the means of knowing God.

f 2:7 See John 13:34–35.

g 2:8 This commandment to love one another is both old and new. It is found in the Old and in you, because the darkness is disappearing and the true light is already blazing.[a]

[9]Anyone who says, "I am in the light," while holding hatred in his heart toward a fellow believer is still in the darkness. [10]But the one who truly loves a fellow believer lives in the light, and there is nothing in him that will cause someone else to stumble.[b] [11]But whoever hates a fellow believer lives in the darkness—stumbling around in the dark with no clue where he is going, for he is blinded by the darkness.[c]

Three Stages of Spiritual Maturity

[12]I remind you, dear children:[d] your sins have been permanently removed because of the power of his name.[e]

[13]I remind you, fathers *and mothers:*[f] you have a relationship with the one who has existed from the beginning.[g]

And I remind you, young people: you have defeated the evil one.[h]

[14]I write these things to you, dear children, because you truly have a relationship with the Father. I write these things, fathers *and mothers,* because

---

Testament (Leviticus 19:18), but it is made radically new and fresh by the teaching of Christ and its application through our lives.

a 2:8 See John 1:5, 9; 8:12. The true light is the revelation of God that shines through Christ. The Aramaic can be translated "The new commandment I write to you became realized in him (Christ) and is in you, destroying the darkness and revealing the light of truth anew."

b 2:10 Or "No fear of stumbling haunts him" or "There is no trap laid for him."

c 2:11 John is equating darkness with the absence of love. To love is to walk in God's light. To hate is to walk in darkness.

d 2:12 The Greek word for "child," *teknion,* is a child still in training (under instruction), with an implication of servanthood.

e 2:12 That is, through faith in who Christ is and what he has done to redeem us through the blood of his sacrifice.

f 2:13 Fathers and mothers (parents) are not necessarily "old men" and "old women," but those who reproduce and raise children.

g 2:13 That is, Christ. See John 1:1 and 1 John 1:1-3. Nothing more is said about fathers and mothers other than knowing Christ, for what could be more important than that?

h 2:13 Our enemy, Satan, is defeated through our union with Christ as we share in the triumphs of his cross and resurrection, the word of our testimony, the blood of the Lamb, and by not loving our own lives. See Revelation 12:10.

you have had a true relationship with him who is from the beginning. And I write these things, young people, because you are strong, the Word of God is treasured in your hearts, and you have defeated the evil one.[a]

A Warning Not to Love the World

[15]Don't set the affections of your heart on this world[b] or in loving the things of the world. The love of the Father and the love of the world are incompatible.[c] [16]For all that the world can offer us—the gratification of our flesh, the allurement of the things of the world, and the obsession with status and importance[d]—none of these things comes from the Father but from the world. [17]This world[e] and its desires are in the process of passing away, but those who *love to*[f] do the will of God live forever.[g]

Believing in Jesus

[18]Dear children, the end *of this age* is near! You have heard that Antichrist is arising,[h] and in fact, many enemies of Christ have already appeared, and this

---

a 2:14 John gives young people (in Hebrew culture this would be anyone under forty) the three main components of spiritual growth: 1) courageous faith, 2) loving the Word of God, and 3) defeating the Evil One through our union with Christ.

b 2:15 Or "Stop loving the world system (the ways of the world)."

c 2:15 Or "If anyone persists in loving the world, there is no love for the Father in him."

d 2:16 These are the three areas of temptation that the serpent used with Adam and Eve in the garden to pull them away from the Father and what the Devil used to tempt Jesus in the wilderness. He is an expert at using these cravings to dilute our love for the Father and cause us to turn our affections to the things of this life. See Genesis 3:6 and Matthew 4:1–11. But the values of the kingdom of God are: setting our affections on things above, living in the fruit of the Spirit (self-control), and humility, which always waits for God's timing for promotion.

e 2:17 That is, the world system and the desire to be in a world system that leaves God out of the picture are disappearing. Planet Earth is not fading away here, but the systems, structure, and world order are.

f 2:17 Implied in the Greek present-tense verb, which means "to continually (habitually) do the will of God."

g 2:17 There is an interesting word play in the Aramaic in this verse. The Aramaic word for "world" is *alma*, and the word for "forever" is *alam*.

h 2:18 The Greek verb *erchomai* can be translated "to come, to become known, to be established, to appear, to show oneself, to arise."

is how we know that we are living in the closing hour *of this age.*[a] [19]*For even though they were once a part of us,* they withdrew from us because they were never really of our number. For if they had truly belonged to us they would have continued with us.[b] By leaving our community of believers they made it obvious that they never really belonged to us.[c]

[20]But the Holy One has anointed you and you all know *the truth.*[d] [21]So I'm writing you not because you don't know the truth, but because you do know it, and no lie belongs to the truth.[e]

The Power of the Truth

[22]Who is the real liar but the one who denies that Jesus is the Christ. He is the real antichrist, the one who denies the Father and the Son.[f] [23]Whoever rejects the Son rejects the Father. Whoever embraces[g] the Son embraces the Father also. [24]So you must be sure to keep the message burning[h] in your hearts; that is, the message *of life* you heard from the beginning. If you do,

---

a 2:18 The final hour is John's description of what Paul describes as the "last days." The final hour or last days began at Pentecost (Acts 2:16–17; Hebrews 1:2). We have been living in the last days for more than two thousand years. In these last days many antichrists will come. They oppose the teachings of Christ, lead people astray, and separate from the true community of Christ followers. There is no one individual named "*the* antichrist (or enemy of Christ)" in the Bible. (The definite article *the* is never used in connection to antichrist (or "anti-anointing"). John tells us that the "spirit of antichrist" has already been in the world (1 John 4:3) and that many antichrists (false teachers who oppose the truth of Christ and have a following) have already come. John's warning is that we must set our hearts firmly on the truths of Jesus Christ and his word as protection from the multiple errors that will increasingly try to deceive believers. The words *antichrist* and *antichrists* are not found in the book of Revelation but only in 1 and 2 John.

b 2:19 The Aramaic is "They would have clung to us" or "remained tied to us."

c 2:19 Or "All of them do not belong to us." Apparently they were not thrown out of the church or excommunicated but left of their own accord. See also 1 John 4:5.

d 2:20 Or "You (have the capacity to) know all things."

e 2:21 Jesus is the New Reality and the Truth. See John 14:6.

f 2:22 We have here the definition of *antichrist.* It is anyone who denies the Son (or denies that Jesus is the anointed Messiah). To deny Christ is to reject the Father, who gave him to us to reveal who the Father truly is. The Father and the Son are one; you cannot receive one and reject the other.

g 2:23 Or "confesses."

h 2:24 Or "residing in you."

you will always be living in close fellowship with the Son and with the Father. [25]And he himself has promised us the never-ending life of the ages to come!

[26]I've written these things about those who are attempting to lead you astray. [27]But the wonderful anointing you have received from God[a] *is so much greater than their deception and* now lives in you. There's no need for anyone to keep teaching you.[b] His anointing teaches you all that you need to know, for it will lead you into truth, not a counterfeit. So just as the anointing has taught you, remain in him.[c]

[28]And now, dear children, remain in him, so that when he is revealed we may have joyful confidence and not be ashamed when we stand before him at his appearing.[d]

[29]If you know that he is righteous, you may be sure that everyone who lives in righteousness has been divinely fathered by him.[e]

Three

Divine Sonship

[1]Look with wonder at the depth of the Father's marvelous love that he has

---

a 2:27 Although absent in the Greek, the words "from God" are found in the Aramaic manuscripts. It is clear from the context that the "anointing" is the Holy Spirit poured into us, bringing life, illumination, wisdom, fruit, and power from the indwelling life of Christ.

b 2:27 Or "There is no need for anyone to keep teaching you his opinions (deceptions)." John is not telling them not to continue to be taught the Word of God, for God has placed teachers in the church to instruct us and equip us and bring us into the fullness of Christ (1 Corinthians 12:28; Ephesians 4:11; Hebrews 13:7, 17). John's warning concerns those who lead us astray by the false doctrines of men. The bride of Christ will always need Holy Spirit–filled teachers who illuminate us in the ways of Christ.

c 2:27 The Greek can be translated "remain in him (Christ)" or "remain in it (the anointing)."

d 2:28 See also Luke 16:3; 2 Corinthians 10:8; Philippians 1:20; 1 Peter 4:16.

e 2:29 Or "born of him." Living in righteousness, or doing what is right before God, is the proof that we have been fathered by God himself.

lavished on us! He has called us and made us his very own *beloved* children.[a] The reason the world doesn't recognize who we are is that they didn't recognize him.[b] [2]Beloved, we are God's children right now; however, it is not yet apparent what we will become. But we do know that when it[c] is finally made visible,[d] we will be just like him, for we will see him as he truly is. [3]And all who focus their hope on him will always be purifying[e] themselves,[f] just as Jesus is pure.[g]

The Character of God's Children

[4]Anyone who indulges in sin[h] lives in moral anarchy, for *the definition of sin is breaking God's law.*[i] [5]And you know without a doubt that Jesus was revealed to eradicate sins, and there is no sin in him. Anyone who continues to live in union with him will not sin. [6]But the one who continues sinning[j] hasn't seen him *with discernment* or known him *by intimate experience.*

---

a 3:1 As translated from the Aramaic. The Greek reads "that we should be called God's children, and indeed we are." See Romans 8:14–17; Galatians 3:26–27; 4:6–7.

b 3:1 That is, Jesus, God incarnated in human form.

c 3:2 The Aramaic can be translated "It has not been revealed until now what we are destined to be." Many translations view the subject of the Greek verb *phanerōthē* to be Christ ("when *he* is revealed"), but in the immediate context, "what we will be" becomes the subject and makes better grammatical sense.

d 3:2 The Greek word *phaneroō* means "to make clear, to be made visible," and it comes from the verb *phainō*, which means "to shine." John is saying we are not yet shining as we will one day. We are both children of God and reflections of God. See Daniel 12:3.

e 3:3 The Greek word *hagnizo* is found only twice in the New Testament. John uses the term in John 11:55 to refer to ritually cleansing ourselves in order to be morally undefiled as we come into God's presence.

f 3:3 There is a purifying hope that transforms us. This is more than the Second Coming. This is the hope of glory, that we will be revealed as fully like Christ. See Colossians 1:25–27.

g 3:3 Or "as that one (Jesus) is pure." The beautiful purity of Jesus' life is the model for our lives.

h 3:4 Or "who habitually sins."

i 3:4 The Aramaic is "Whoever commits sin commits evil, for sin is absolutely evil."

j 3:6 The present tense of the Greek verb throughout this section indicates a behavior that is persistent and habitual. John is not speaking of those who are yet to walk in complete victory, but those who continue sinning and find ways to excuse and justify it.

⁷Delightfully loved children, don't let anyone divert you from this truth. The person who keeps doing what is right *proves that he* is righteous before God, even as the Messiah[a] is righteous. ⁸But the one who indulges in a sinful life is of the Devil,[b] because the Devil has been sinning from the beginning. The reason the Son of God was revealed was to undo and destroy the works of the Devil.

⁹Everyone who is truly God's child will refuse to keep sinning[c] because God's seed[d] remains within him, and he is unable to continue sinning because he has been fathered by God himself.[e] ¹⁰Here is how God's children can be clearly distinguished from the children of the Evil One.[f] Anyone who does not demonstrate righteousness[g] and show love to fellow believers is not living with God as his source.[h]

Love One Another

¹¹The beautiful message you've heard right from the start is that we should walk in self-sacrificing love toward one another.¹²We should not be like Cain, who yielded to the Evil One and brutally murdered his own brother, Abel.[i] And why did he murder him? Because his own actions were evil and his brother's righteous.

¹³So don't be shocked, beloved brothers and sisters, if you experience the world's hatred. ¹⁴Yet we can be assured that we have been translated from *spiritual* death into *spiritual* life because we love the family of believers.

---

a 3:7 As translated from the Aramaic.

b 3:8 Or "is operating under the influence of the Devil." That is, belonging to the Devil, not to Christ.

c 3:9 The Aramaic is "never serves sin."

d 3:9 This is the Greek word *sperma*, "male seed." See 2 Peter 1:4.

e 3:9 Or "born of God." We have been fathered by God himself and we carry his DNA, his genes.

f 3:10 Or "children of the Devil (Adversary)." This is the only place in the New Testament that refers to those who have never experienced salvation as the Devil's children. See also John 8:44.

g 3:10 Or "justice."

h 3:10 Or "is not of God."

i 3:11 See Genesis 4:8–10.

A loveless life remains spiritually dead. [15]Everyone who keeps hating a fellow believer is a murderer,[a] and you know that no murderer has eternal life residing in him.

[16]This is how we have discovered love's reality: Jesus sacrificed his life for us.[b] Because of this great love, we should be willing to lay down our lives for one another. [17]If anyone sees a fellow believer in need and has the means to help him, yet shows no pity and closes his heart against him, how is it even possible that God's love lives in him?[c]

[18]Beloved children, our love can't be an abstract theory we only talk about, but a way of life demonstrated through our loving deeds. [19]We know that the truth lives within us[d] because we demonstrate love in action, which will reassure[e] our hearts in his presence.[f]

[20]Whenever our hearts make us feel guilty *and remind us of our failures*, we know that God is much greater *and more merciful* than our conscience, and he knows everything there is to know *about us*.[g] [21]My delightfully loved friends, when our hearts don't condemn us, we have a bold freedom to speak face-to-face with God. [22]And whatever we ask of him we receive,[h] because we keep his commands. And by our beautiful intentions[i] we continue to do what brings pleasure to him.

---

a 3:15 See Matthew 5:21–22.

b 3:16 Or "that he (Jesus) placed his soul over us and we are constantly indebted to place our souls over our brothers and sisters."

c 3:16 Real love is an action. Think of God's love, which rescues, saves, and empowers. Love is more like a verb than a noun. Love is seen by actions, not just words.

d 3:19 Or "that we are of (belong to) the truth."

e 3:19 Or "tranquilize our hearts."

f 3:19 The Aramaic can be translated "By this we recognize that we are of the truth and make our hearts confident (or deliver our hearts) before he comes."

g 3:20 There is a higher courtroom for the human heart: it is where grace is enthroned. The very worst that is in us is known by God and he still showers mercy, love, and acceptance upon us. This is the greatness of God's grace. He sees beyond the sin of a moment and sees the holy affections of love in those who refuse to turn away from him. See John 21:17.

h 3:21 See Matthew 7:7, 21:22; John 9:31, 14:13–14; 15:7.

i 3:22 As translated from the Aramaic.

²³So these are his commands: that we continually place our trust in the name of his Son, Jesus Christ, and that we keep loving one another, just as he has commanded us. ²⁴For all who obey his commands find their lives joined in union with him, and he lives and flourishes in them. We know and have proof that he constantly lives and flourishes in us, by the Spirit that he has given us.

Four

A Warning Against False Teaching

¹Delightfully loved friends, don't trust every spirit, but carefully examine *what they say*^a to determine if they are of God, because many false prophets have mingled into the world. ²Here's the test for those with the genuine Spirit of God: they will confess Jesus as the Christ who has come in the flesh.^b ³Everyone who does not acknowledge that Jesus is from God has the spirit of antichrist, which you heard was coming and is already active in the world.

⁴Little children, you can be certain that you belong to God and have conquered them,^c for the one who is living in you is far greater than the one who is in the world.^d ⁵They belong to this world and they articulate the spirit of this world, and the world listens to them. ⁶But we belong to God, and whoever truly knows God listens to us. Those who refuse to listen to us do

---

a 4:1 Although "what they say" is implied, it is clear that John is speaking of those who prophesy, and it is made explicit by the mention of false prophets.

b 4:2 Or "confesses that Jesus Christ has come in the flesh."

c 4:4 That is, the antichrists who deny that Jesus is the Christ.

d 4:4 That is, the Devil. We have the Word of God, the Holy Spirit, the favor of God, and Jesus Christ. Within us is more than enough power to overcome the evil in this world. John uses the word "world" (Gr. *kosmos*) more than any other New Testament writer (104 times) to convey the concept of this world system or world order. One could describe it as "the culture of the world."

not belong to God. That is how we can know the difference between the spirit of truth and the spirit of deceit.[a]

God Is Love

[7]Those who are loved by God, let his love continually pour from you to one another, because God is love. Everyone who loves is fathered by God and experiences an intimate knowledge of him. [8]The one who doesn't love has yet to know God, for God is love.[b] [9]The light of God's love shined within us[c] when he sent his matchless[d] Son into the world so that we might live through him.[e] [10]This is love:[f] He loved us *long before we loved him*. It was his love, not ours. He proved it by sending his Son to be the pleasing sacrificial offering to take away our sins.[g]

---

a 4:6 The New Testament gives us a number of ways we can discern true prophets from false ones. John gives us eight here: 1) They must confess that Jesus the Messiah has come in bodily form (vv. 2–3); 2) They must not come in the spirit of this world (v. 5); 3) They must listen to the truth (v. 6); 4) They must demonstrate love (vv. 7–21); 5) The Spirit of Truth must be in them (vv. 4–6); 6) They must remain true to the written Word of God (v. 6; 5:10; 2 Timothy 3:16); 7) They must be overcomers who have the greater One living in them (v. 4); 8) They must have a commitment to the body of Christ (2:19).

b 4:8 and 4:16 Or "God continually exists, being love."

c 4:8 Or "God's love was revealed among us." The base word for "revealed" is *phainō,* "to shine light."

d 4:9 Or "only begotten." That is, Jesus had no beginning and was the eternal Son of God as part of the triune essence or Godhead.

e 4:9 The Aramaic is "that we might live in his hand," considered to be an idiom for living by his grace.

f 4:10 The Aramaic is "This is how love was born."

g 4:10 The Greek term *hilasmos* can be described as "a cleansing, satisfying sacrifice that provides a covering shelter." A form of the word is used for "mercy seat" in Hebrews 9:5. God's love provides the answer for life's greatest questions: 1) Why was I created? To receive and experience God's love. 2) Does God care about me? God's love is indiscriminate; he loves everyone and cares about every detail of our lives. 3) Am I really free to choose or reject God's love? Yes—love must be a choice, freely and without compulsion. 4) What is the way of salvation? Love became a man and died as our sacrificial offering to bring us the free gift of salvation. 5) How can I really know that I am saved? When we respond with faith to God's loving invitation and then demonstrate it by loving others, we have the assurance of our salvation. 6) How can I know that God loves me? His love prompted him to send his unique and beautiful Son to the earth to be our Savior and Redeemer. He offers to everyone the invitation to experience even deeper measures of

[11]Delightfully loved ones, if he loved us with such tremendous love, then "loving one another" should be our way of life! [12]No one has ever gazed[a] upon the fullness of God's splendor.[b] But if we love one another, God makes his permanent home in us, and we make our permanent home in him, and his love is brought to its full expression in us. [13]And he has given us his Spirit within us so that we can have the assurance that he lives in us and that we live in him.

[14]Moreover, we have seen with our own eyes and can testify to the truth that Father God has sent his Son to be the Savior of the world. [15]Those who give thanks[c] that Jesus is the Son of God live in God, and God lives in them. [16]We have come into an intimate experience with God's love, and we trust in the love he has for us.[d]

God is love! Those who are living in love are living in God, and God lives through them. [17]By *living in God*,[e] love has been brought to its full expression in us[f] so that we may fearlessly face the Day of Judgment,[g] because all that Jesus now Is,[h] so are we in this world. [18]Love never brings fear, for fear is always related to punishment. But love's perfection drives the fear *of punishment far* from our hearts. Whoever walks constantly afraid of

---

his love. And he gives us his Holy Spirit as confirmation that he loves and cherishes us and gives us the power to love others. See Ephesians 3:14–21.

a 4:12 Or "watched." The Greek verb *theaomai* is used in classical Greek for "watching a play or spectator sport."

b 4:12 See John 1:18; 5:37; 6:46.

c 4:15 As translated from the Aramaic.

d 4:16 Or "in us."

e 4:17 Or "by this (relationship with God)."

f 4:17 Or "Love has reached its goal/destiny within us."

g 4:17 The Aramaic is "We will have open faces on the day of judgment." For the true believer filled with God's love, the day of judgment is not to be feared but looked forward to, for perfect love will have made us completely like Christ. Love provides us with no reason to fear the future or to fear punishment from God. See 1 Corinthians 4:5.

h 4:17 Or "because we are what he is in this world." The verb tense is important. We are not like Jesus *was*, but because of grace, we are like he is now: pure and holy, seated in heaven, and glorified. See Romans 8:30; Ephesians 2:6; Colossians 3:1–4. Faith has transferred his righteousness to us.

punishment[a] has not reached love's perfection. [19]Our love for others is *our grateful response* to the love God first demonstrated to us.[b]

[20]Anyone can say, "I love God," yet have hatred toward another believer. This makes him a phony, because if you don't love a brother or sister, whom you can see, how can you truly love God, whom you can't see? [21]For he has given us this command: whoever loves God must also demonstrate love to others.[c]

Five

The Proof of Love and the Victory of Faith

[1]Everyone who believes that Jesus is the Messiah is God's spiritual child and has been fathered by God himself. And everyone who loves Father God loves his children as well. [2]This is how we can be sure that we love the children of God: by having a passionate love for God and by obedience to his commands. [3]True love for God means obeying his commands, and his commands don't weigh us down as heavy burdens.[d] [4]*You see,* every child of God overcomes[e] the world, for our faith is the victorious power that triumphs over the world. [5]So who are the world conquerors, *defeating its power?* Those who believe that Jesus is the Son of God.

---

a 4:18 The immediate context shows that it is the implied fear of correction, punishment, or rejection. The Aramaic is "Fear is suspicious."

b 4:19 Or "We (continue to) love because God first loved us." Some manuscripts read, "We love God because he first loved us."

c 4:21 The real proof of our love for God must always be in how we express love and treat others with dignity and respect, esteeming them in love.

d 5:3 God's grace empowers us to love, which makes his commands a delight instead of a duty. The spontaneity of love is never crushed by the commands of a loving God.

e 5:4 The Greek verb tense indicates continuous action, "continually conquers the world (system)."

The Spirit, the Water, and the Blood

[6]Jesus Christ is the one who was revealed *as God's Son* by his water *baptism* and by the blood *of his cross*—not by water only, but by water and blood.[a] And the Spirit, who is truth, confirms this with his testimony. [7]So we have these three constant witnesses giving their evidence:[b] [8]the Spirit, the water, and the blood. And these three are in agreement. [9]If we accept the testimony of men, *how much more should we accept* the more authoritative testimony of God that he has testified concerning his Son?

[10]Those who believe in the Son of God have the *living* testimony in their hearts. Those who don't believe have made God out to be a liar by not believing the testimony God has confirmed about his Son. This is the true testimony: that God has given us eternal life, and this life has its source in his Son.[c] Whoever has the Son has *eternal* life; whoever does not have the Son does not possess *eternal* life.

Assurance of Eternal Life

[13]I've written this letter to you who believe in the name of the Son of God so that you will *be assured and* know without a doubt that you have eternal life.

[15]Since we have this confidence, we can also have great boldness before him, for if we present any request agreeable to his will, he will hear us. And

---

a 5:6 At Jesus' baptism the voice of the Father acknowledged him as his beloved Son. At the cross his blood was shed to bring the reality of Christ to those who believe in him. The majority view of current scholarship is this passage refers to Jesus' baptism and the cross. It is possible, however, that John is referring to the blood and water that spilled from the side of Jesus after his death.

b 5:7 There is considerable historical and theological debate surrounding verses 7–8. Some later, less reliable manuscripts have for verse 7: "There are three that testify in heaven: the Father, the Word, and the Holy Spirit. And these three are one." This is known as the *Comma Johanneum*. But there has been a nearly complete agreement of scholars that this reading was added by copyists, with many theories of who it was. Although there is nothing heretical about this addition, it seems to have been inserted to reinforce the doctrine of the Trinity. It is not included in modern versions nor in the Aramaic.

c 5:11 Or "This life is in (as connected to him as source) his Son." It can also mean that God has placed us in life union with his Son to manifest eternal life in us.

if we know that he hears us in whatever we ask, we also know that we have obtained the requests we ask of him.

[16]If anyone observes a fellow believer habitually sinning in a way that doesn't lead to death,[a] you should keep interceding in prayer that God will give that person life. Now, there is a sin that leads to death, and I'm not encouraging you to pray for those who commit it. [17]All unrighteousness is sin, but there is sin that does not result in death.

[18]We are convinced that everyone fathered by God does not make sinning a way of life, because the Son of God protects the child of God, and the evil one cannot touch him. [19]We know that we are God's children and that the whole world lies under the misery and influence of the Evil One. [20]And we know that the Son of God has made our understanding come alive so that we can know by experience the one who is true. And we are in him who is true, God's Son, Jesus Christ—the true God and eternal life!

[21]So, little children, guard yourselves from worshipping anything but him.[b]

---

a 5:16 That is, if the sinning is persisted in, it may lead to death. Some believe this may refer to the unforgivable sin of blasphemy of the Holy Spirit (Matthew 12:31–32; Mark 3:28–30; Luke 12:8–10), or possibly the sin that brings death in taking communion "unworthily" (1 Corinthians 11:27–30), or lying to the Holy Spirit (Acts 5:1–11). However, John speaks in this letter about the gross apostasy of those who turn away from the truth and depart from the fellowship of believers and follow the teaching of antichrists.

b 5:21 Or "Keep yourselves from idols." The Aramaic is "Keep your souls from fear of idols."

2 John

LOVING TRUTH

Translator's Introduction to 2 John

AT A GLANCE

Author: The apostle John

Audience: Communities in Asia Minor experiencing schism

Date: AD 85-90

Type of Literature: A letter

Major Themes: Truth, brotherly love, and false teachers

Outline:

    Letter Opening — 1-3
    An Exhortation to Walk in Truth and Love — 4-6
    A Warning Against False Teachers — 7-11
    Letter Closing — 12-13

ABOUT 2 JOHN

The book of 2 John points us to the truth and encourages us to hold it fast and never let it go. The theme of John's second letter could be described as "Loving Truth." Truth generates love, and love will always be faithful to the truth. To love God is to love his truth and cherish it in our hearts.

    Some scholars believe that John penned what we've called his second letter actually first, before 1 John. Given that it addresses the same heart-breaking situation of schisms over false teaching that were wreaking the fragile churches under John's care in Asia Minor, some see this as a quick, almost hurriedly written note from the heart of a spiritual father to his children in trouble. Then he followed up his initial warnings with a second letter (which we know as 1 John) to make a greater appeal and guard their ongoing spiritual lives. Others see in this letter a follow-up to the first one, possibly written to a more distant audience, or even as a cover letter to 1 John given its personal greetings.

Regardless, what's evident is that John was deeply burdened for the chaos being caused in his network of churches. This beloved disciple of Jesus wanted his beloved disciples to experience the pure, living truth that had made a home in them. He also wanted them to walk in love, for to walk in love is to walk in the truth of God.

John's letter will bring a fresh understanding of God to your heart. Let him speak to you through his faithful servant John. Enjoy!

PURPOSE

As with his first letter, John wrote to the communities to which he was an overseer ("the elder" is a title suggesting spiritual authority) with one singular purpose: to guard and protect them from the false teachers who had gone out into them and were deceiving them. These were itinerant teachers who were bearing a "truth" contrary to the received Spirit-anointed truth of the gospel. He writes as a spiritual father who was concerned about schisms wreaking his beloved children.

AUTHOR AND AUDIENCE

While the letter only identifies the author as "the elder," it's clear he was in a position of spiritual authority over his community and wrote in a similar manner and tone as both 1 John and the gospel of John. Given this, it's no surprise that the tradition from the earliest days of the church assumed the apostle John authored the letter. Though the text doesn't bear his name, early leaders like Polycarp and Papias both ascribed it to him.

Possibly written earlier than his first letter, John addressed this one to "the chosen woman" and "her children." Most commentators see this as a metaphor for the church with its spiritual believers (children), believing that John the Elder wrote the letter to a church or network of churches. Some have viewed it more literally as written to an unnamed woman or a woman named Electa or Kyria (feminine of *kurios*, "lord"). Regardless of who the letter was written to, it is inspired of God to bring truth to our hearts and keep us from evil.

MAJOR THEMES

Walking and Staying in the Truth. As with his first letter, John is concerned with the truth of the gospel—not only that believers guard it, but also walk in it and stay in it. The living truth of Christ has a permanent home in our lives, and will stay with us for all eternity. But we're also commanded to actively walk in the truth and stay in the truth—because as John says, "Anyone who wanders away and does not remain faithful to the teaching of Christ has no relationship with God" (9). For it's only when we continue in the truth that we have intimate connection with both the Father and the Son.

Loving One Another. Not only are we to love truth, we're to love each other. After all, this isn't a new command but one we've had from the beginning of time—and one our Lord and Savior Jesus Christ himself gave us. Loving one another means following the commands of Christ, which are always directed both upward (to God) and outward (to others). When we love our neighbor as ourselves, we are also loving the God who made them and saved them!

Warning about False Teachers. Finally, John warned against "deceivers" who might come into our midst and go beyond the teachings of Christ—trying to drag us with them. Early on, some believers thought this letter had either been a cover letter to 1 John, or an appendix added to its end. This makes sense given its close connection with John's first letter warning against false teachers. John reiterates our need to watch out for such antichrists—going so far as to instruct us not even to show hospitality to them, for anyone who welcomes them shares in their wicked work.

2 John

Loving Truth

[1]From the elder[a] to God's chosen woman[b] and her children:

I love you all *as those who are* in the truth.[c] And I'm not the only one, for all who come to know the truth[d] share my love for you [2]because of the *living* truth that has a permanent home in us and will be with us forever.[e]

[3]God our Father and Jesus Christ, his Son, will release to us *overflowing* grace, mercy, and peace, filled with true love.[f]

[4]I was delighted and filled with joy when I learned that your children are

---

a 1 Or "presbyter." This was obviously a self-designated term for the apostle John. He was an elder because of being the only living apostle who was chosen by Jesus.

b 1 The letter is addressed to the *eklekte kuria* ("elect/chosen/excellent lady"). Most commentators see this as a metaphor for the church and her spiritual children, believing that John wrote this letter to a sister congregation or network of congregations. This has been the majority view since it was first noted by Jerome (Jerome Ex. Xi. Ad Ageruchiam). Still, others see it as a letter to a specific woman, with the conjecture that her name was either Elekta or Kyria. This is a possibility, since one way to read the letter is that John knew this woman and was acquainted with her sister and her children (v. 13). If this was indeed written to Kyria (feminine of "lord," meaning a woman in authority), there is a possibility that she was the pastor or overseer of a specific church. But who was the "most especially chosen woman" in the entire Bible? It was Mary, the mother of our Lord Jesus. John was given the commission by Jesus himself in his last moments on earth to care for Mary as his mother, and we know that Mary had a sister (John 19:25–27, cp. v. 13). What other woman is chosen and loved, not only by John but all the church? Every believer in Jesus rightly honors and reveres his mother, Mary. Throughout church history there have been a few scholars who believe that Mary was the recipient of this letter. See Knauer (Stud. U. Krit., 1833, Part 2, p.452ff; q.v. J. E. Huther, *Critical and Exegetical Handbook to the General Epistles of James, Peter, John, and Jude*, translated from the German, 11 vols., Funk and Wagnalls, 1884).

c 1 Or "whom I love in truth." John uses the word *love* sixty-two times in the New Testament, while all the other New Testament writers combined use it a total of 116 times.

d 1 It is possible that John is using the word *truth* as he uses *word* ("logos"), as a title for Jesus Christ ("all who know the Truth").

e 2 Or "into the age." The Aramaic is "because the truth sustains us to the end of the eternity."

f 3 Or "in truth and love."

consistently living in the truth, just as we have received the command from the Father.

⁵Dearest woman, I have a request to make of you. It is not a new commandment but a repetition of the one we have had from the beginning: that we constantly love one another. ⁶This love means living in obedience to whatever God commands us. For to walk in love toward one another is the unifying commandment we've heard from the beginning.

Warning about False Teachers

⁷Numerous deceivers have surfaced *from among us* and gone out into the world,ᵃ people who will not acknowledge Jesus Christ coming as a man. These deceivers are antichrists! ⁸Be on your guard so that you do not lose all that weᵇ have *diligently* worked for but receive a full reward.

⁹Anyone who wanders awayᶜ and does not remain faithful to the teaching of Christ has no relationship with God. But those who remain in the teaching of Christ have a *wonderful* relationship with both the Father and the Son. ¹⁰So if anyone comes *into your fellowship claiming to be a true believer* yet doesn't bring this teaching, you are not to consider him as a fellow believer,ᵈ nor should you welcome him into your homes.ᵉ ¹¹For if you welcome him as a believer,ᶠ you will be partnering with him in his evil agenda.

¹²Although I have many more subjects I'd like to discuss with you, I'd rather not include them in this letter.ᵍ But I look forward to coming to visit

---

a 7 In the context of love, John now mentions false teachers. This shows us that love is the safeguard against error. The more that love flows through us as we honor God's commands, the more we are kept from deception. Our unity, produced by love, enables us to recognize and resist false teachers.

b 8 Some manuscripts have "you."

c 9 Or "goes beyond (the teaching of Christ)." The Aramaic implies a visiting minister or itinerant speaker: "whoever passes through."

d 10 Or "Don't give him any greeting (as a believer)." Hospitality was such a cultural virtue in the time of John that he actually had to warn them not to show hospitality to false teachers.

e 10 Or possibly "house (church)."

f 11 Or "if you give him a (public) greeting (as a believer)."

g 12 Or "I'd rather not write with ink (pen) and paper."

and speaking with you face-to-face[a]—for being together will complete our joy!

[13] The children of your sister, whom God has chosen, send you their loving greetings. Amen.[b]

a 12 The Aramaic is "mouth to mouth."
b 13 Most manuscripts do not include "Amen."

3 John

LOVE IN ACTION

Translator's Introduction to 3 John

AT A GLANCE

Author: The apostle John

Audience: Gaius, a friend of John

Date: AD 85–90

Type of Literature: A letter

Major Themes: Truth, hospitality, divisiveness, and doing good

Outline:

    Letter Opening — 1–4
    An Exhortation to Show Hospitality — 5–8
    An Example of Inhospitality — 9–11
    Letter Closing — 12–13

ABOUT 3 JOHN

Though it is the smallest of the New Testament letters, this piece of ancient correspondence offers us a glimpse into a problem every modern church should consider: hospitality, especially for those called and anointed by Christ as ministers of his gospel.

    There's a good chance that one of the characters in the letter, Demetrius, was himself a missionary who was associated with the apostle John and actually carried it as a sort of letter of introduction to the letter's recipient, Gaius. This dear man was known to John as a faithful host for missionaries who were spreading the gospel in the region. One can imagine Gaius rolling out the red carpet, breaking out the fine china, and making up an extra bed for Christ's emissaries who were tirelessly working on behalf of the Lord. Oh to be known for being a welcoming spirit, and for pouring out love and support for the sake of others! And woe to the one who denies hospitality and stirs up trouble within the body, which is exactly what one of the other characters had done.

John's motivation for penning and sending his letter to the small community in modern Turkey (Asia Minor) was to commend hospitality as a way of expression Christian love. John was thrilled at how Gaius had welcomed traveling evangelists throughout the region, and he wanted him to continue this show of support. John's letter will bring a fresh understanding of God to your heart. Let him speak to you through his faithful servant John. Enjoy!

PURPOSE

John's third letter, similar in structure and vocabulary as 2 John, was more of a general letter sent to the churches scattered throughout Turkey (Asia Minor), even as it was addressed to one leader of one local community. John wrote to them to encourage them to welcome itinerant minsters who would travel and teach the different congregations—commending a particularly hospitable church leader, Gaius. He also warned against allowing pride and self-centeredness to get in the way of showing such love and support. It is a letter of hospitality and carries John's trademark truths of showing love and grace to all.

AUTHOR AND AUDIENCE

This intimate letter between Christian brothers addressing a situation in a local church involved four people: "the elder," who sent the note; Gaius, who received the letter; and Diotrephes and Demetrius, church leaders in the region mentioned in the letter. Though various suggestions have been offered as to the identity of this elder, as with 2 John early Christians identified him as the apostle John, beloved disciple of Jesus. Although he wrote to one church leader in Asia Minor, the letter may have been intended for a wider audience to encourage them to continue to support missionaries bearing the gospel of Christ with open-armed hospitality.

MAJOR THEMES

Walking in the Truth. This is a common theme in John's letters, walking in the truth of Christ. Such walking is not only a joyful experience for those who are spiritually responsibly for others (like parents when they see their children walking with Christ). It's also a joyful experience for believers, whose souls get along well in spiritual health as they maintain their commitment to Jesus in words and deeds.

Showing Christian Hospitality. True hospitality is a lost art in some churches today and must be valued. Gaius stands as an example to us all of how it looks to faithfully demonstrate loving hospitality to our fellow brothers and sisters in Christ—especially when it comes to ministers of the gospel, who deserve our full, generous support. True Christian commitment to truth means a commitment to love through support.

Divisiveness within the Body. One of the greatest toxins to the body of Christ is divisiveness—whether that's a division in truth that false teachers bring, or a division in love that problem believers create. Such an attitude manifests itself in pride, inhospitality, gossip, slander, malice, and obstruction. Not only did John warn against such people, he warned against imitating them within the body. We should name them and call such people out—just as John did with Diotrephes.

Doing and Imitating Good. "Don't imitate what is evil," John wrote, "but imitate that which is good" (11). John reveals something important about what we are to imitate: the *good* here is not just any good, but godly good. It's goodness reflecting God's good character and good acts, built on his inspiring love. Such people not only prove they are of God, but those who don't prove they've never been in relationship with him in the first place.

3 John

Love in Action

[1]From the elder[a] to my dearly loved brother Gaius,[b] whom I truly love:[c]

[2]Beloved friend, I pray that you are prospering in every way[d] and that you continually enjoy good health, just as your soul is prospering.[e]

[3]I was filled with joy and delight when the brothers arrived and informed me of your *faithfulness to the* truth. They told me how you live continually in the truth *of Christ.*[f] [4]It is the greatest joy of my life to hear that my children are consistently living their lives in the ways of truth!

Financially Supporting Missionaries

[5]My beloved friend, *I commend you for your demonstration* of faithful love by all that you have done for the brothers *on their journey,* even though they

---

a 1 Or "presbyter." This was obviously a self-designated term for the apostle John. He was an elder because of being the only living apostle who was chosen by Jesus.

b 1 Gaius was a convert of John's and a close friend who likely had a leadership position in the church (location not given). Church tradition states that he was one of the seventy whom Jesus sent out and was later ordained by John as the bishop of Pergamum. See *Apostolic Constitutions* (7.46.9; Funk 1, 454). However, there was also a Gaius who became the bishop of Ephesus. There are four mentions of Gaius in the New Testament, although it is unlikely that they were the same person (Acts 19:29; Romans 16:23; 1 Corinthians 1:14). The name Gaius means "joyful or happy." The Latin form of *Caius* can be translated "lord."

c 1 Or "continually love in truth (reality)."

d 2 The Greek word *eudōomai* means "to be brought along to a smooth and prosperous journey" or "to be continually prospered (unto success) in every way." The Aramaic is "as much as succeeds you." See Joshua 1:8.

e 2 John is praying that Gaius's physical health would match his spiritual health. God is concerned for both our physical health (he gave our bodies an immune system) and our souls (emotional and spiritual well-being). If physical health and soul "prosperity" were not the will of God, why would John pray that for Gaius?

f 3 Although the word Jesus, or Christ, does not appear anywhere in the text of 3 John, it is clearly implied.

were strangers at the time.[a] [6]They have shared publicly with the congrega-tion[b] about the beautiful acts of love you have shown them.[c] Now, if you would be so kind, send them on their way *with a generous gift*, in a manner that would honor God.[d] [7]You see, it was their passion for *the glory of* the name *of Christ* that launched them out, and they've not accepted financial support from unbelievers.[e] [8]They are deserving of all the support we can give them, *because through our giving* we can partner with them for the truth.[f]

Domineering Diotrephes

[9]I have already written you once about this,[g] but Diotrephes,[h] who loves to be in charge and recognized as first among you, does not acknowledge our authority. [10]So if I come, I will address what he's doing—spreading his

a 5 These are traveling missionaries and itinerant speakers who were shown hospitality by Gaius. True hospitality is a lost art in some churches today and must be valued.

b 6 This would likely have been the church where John was ministering (Ephesus, Per-gamum, or another unnamed location).

c 6 As translated from the Aramaic.

d 6 Or "equal to God's value of them." Apparently, these missionaries had reported to John, returned to the area where Gaius was living, and then continued on with their mis-sionary journey. The Aramaic is quite different: "You outfitted them like a plank billboard for God"; that is, "The gifts you gave them made them an advertisement for God."

e 7 Or "from the Gentiles."

f 8 By giving to those who preach the gospel and nurture the people of God, we are part-nering with them in their ministry.

g 9 This refers to a lost letter, possibly destroyed by Diotrephes. So the letter we now have is actually 4 John.

h 9 Diotrephes was most likely an elder in the congregation who saw himself as the most important one, pushing himself forward with a controlling leadership style. He refused the apostolic authority of John and would not accept guest speakers who may have been sent by John. His name means "nourished by Jupiter." Leaders must view other leaders not as threats but as coworkers. Love is not controlling or tyrannical. It is clear in the New Testament that the local church must have God-appointed ministry in the congregation from pastors, prophets, teachers, evangelists, and apostles (Ephesians 4:11). Additionally, there were itinerant ministries that—if proven authentic—were to be received by the local church authorities and given both opportunities to minister and generous gifts to send them on their way.

malicious slander against us.[a] And not content with that, he refuses to welcome our brothers,[b] and he stands in the way of those who want to receive them and show them hospitality by throwing them out of the church!

[11]Delightfully loved ones, don't imitate what is evil, but imitate that which is good.[c] Whoever does good is of God; whoever does evil has not seen God.[d]

Devoted Demetrius

[12]As for Demetrius, everyone speaks very highly of him,[e] and even the truth itself stands by his side. We too wholeheartedly endorse him, and you know that our recommendation is reliable.

[13]Although I have many more subjects I'd like to discuss with you, I'd rather not include them in this letter.[f] Instead, I hope to visit you and speak with you face-to-face.[g]

[15]Peace to you, *my friend*. Your friends here send their loving greetings to you. Please greet each one of our friends there by name.

---

a 10 Or "with evil words talking nonsense about us."

b 11 These would be the itinerant ministers, missionaries who visited their assembly to minister in the region.

c 11 The Aramaic gives an entirely different slant to this verse. It can be translated "Beloved, don't treat him with malice but with blessing (good deeds)."

d 11 This last clause is asyndetic in order to add emphasis.

e 12 It is possible that Demetrius was one of the "brothers" who was now coming to visit the church and that he was the one who carried this letter to Gaius. This letter served the purpose of being a "letter of recommendation" of Demetrius and his ministry.

f 12 Or "I'd rather not write with ink (pen) and paper."

g 12 The Aramaic is "mouth to mouth."

Jude *(Judah)*

TRUTH WORTH FIGHTING FOR

Translator's Introduction to Jude (Judah)

AT A GLANCE

Author: The apostle Judah, also known as Jude

Audience: Eastern Mediterranean Christians, all God's lovers

Date: AD 58–60

Type of Literature: A letter

Major Themes: Christian faith, Christian life, God's character, salvation, and judgment

Outline:
    Letter Opening — 1–2
    Jude's Reason for Writing — 3–4
    Jude's Arguments Against the False Teachers — 5–16
    Jude's Call to Persevere — 17–23
    Letter Closing — 24–25

ABOUT JUDE (JUDAH)

The name of this book from the Greek text is *Judas,* which is taken from the Hebrew/Aramaic name Judah. The actual name of this book is Judah! One of the most neglected letters in the New Testament, Judah carries a message for every believer today: there is a truth worth fighting for. It is not only writ-ten to you, as one who loves the truth. It is also entrusted to you—to preserve and defend, contend and struggle for.

Though Jude wrote to a specific community who had been influenced by false teachers and foreign ideas to the gospel, his warning to persevere in both believing in our faith and living out our faith is timeless—for the church has always had to contend with false teachers who have tried to pervert the message of God's grace and distort the nature of our salvation.

The one striking fact you'll discover in reading Jude's letter is that he likely refers to two extra-biblical books, *The Assumption of Moses*[a] (v. 9), and the *Book of 1 Enoch* (v. 14–15). This has led some to reject Jude entirely, but there is no law against quoting from non-inspired books or borrowing thoughts and including them in an inspired text. They teach us some import-ant revelation-truths about corruption and ungodliness.

By the last half of the first century there were already many false teach-ers who had infiltrated the ranks of the believers. Jude writes to warn and identify them as those who cause divisions and distort the truths of our faith. Yet you'll find some of the most beautiful treasures in his book, such as pray-ing in the spirit, and the duty of keeping our hearts burning with passion for Jesus. Today, almost two thousand years after Jude wrote his short letter, we still need to guard our hearts and our churches from being led astray from the simplicity of the gospel. After all, these are truths worth fighting for!

PURPOSE

Jude's reason for writing his letter is clear: he needed to urge believers "to vigorously defend and contend for the beliefs that we cherish" (3). Intruders had sown the seeds of false teaching among the believers, creating chaos and confusion. So Jude urged them to preserve, contend, struggle for, and

---

a Or "The Testament of Moses." Some scholars believe *The Assumption of Moses* and *The Testament of Moses* are one in the same. Others see them as different pseudegraphical books.

defend the body of truth we've received from the inspired Word of God, through the teaching ministry of the apostles.

Perhaps to combat and prevent the dangers of the sown heresy from fully blooming, Jude ended his letters by giving seven commands: 1) Keep building up your inner life on the foundation of faith. 2) Pray in the Holy Spirit. 3) Fasten your life to the love of God. 4) Receive more mercy from our Lord Jesus Christ. 5) Have compassion on the wavering. 6) Save the lost. 7) Hate any compromise that will stain our lives. It's when we live the truth of the gospel that we are sure to defend and contend for it most effectively.

AUTHOR AND AUDIENCE

Jude (Judah) is one of the two New Testament books written by half-brothers of Jesus—James and Jude. Jude was possibly the youngest of the four brothers of Jesus (Matthew 13:55). Many scholars believe that Jude may have written his letter only twenty to twenty-five years after the life and resurrection of Jesus (AD 58–60). Although the exact audience is unclear, he most likely was addressing believers who lived in a Greek-speaking area not far from Palestine in the eastern Mediterranean region, including Syria and Egypt. All we know is they had received the gospel from the apostles, and were being disrupted by outsiders who brought ideas foreign to that received teaching.

MAJOR THEMES

Defend and Contend for the Faith. Jude's message reminds us to defend and contend for the faith entrusted to us. It is clear that he is not speaking of faith as simply believing in God, but *the (Christian) faith.* This encompasses the body of truth we receive from the inspired Word of God, delivered by the apostles—the gospel. Jude used an athletic metaphor to drive home the point that we need to struggle as in a great contest, exerting great effort to promote the noble cause of the gospel's advance—while defending these core beliefs, transmitted through generations of Christians, from the threat of false teachers.

Live the Faith. Not only is Jude concerned about the content of the believer's faith, he's also concerned about its expression—for right beliefs and right living go hand-in-hand. The false teachers who had sneaked into the churches were teaching a faith that had "perverted the message of God's grace into a license to commit immorality" (4). Jude feared this perverted message would destroy their beliefs, which would in turn cause them to live ungodly lives. After warning of such examples, he urged believers to live their faith though discipleship, prayer, remaining in God's love, accepting Christ's mercy, compassion, evangelism, and discernment. Living our faith by showing it is the surest way to preserve and contend for it!

The Character of God. Jude offers us a rich understanding of the character and person of God—beginning with the words "chosen," "wrapped in the love," and "kept and guarded." This is what God has done for us who have believed! He is also the God who reveals, for he has entrusted to us revelation-truths through his apostles, leading to our salvation. Then there are shades of the Trinity: he urges believers to pray in the Holy Spirit, remain in God's (the Father's) love, and receive the mercy of Jesus Christ (20–21). Finally, we find one of the most vibrant, almost hymnic descriptions of God at the end in verses 24–25: God keeps us from sin, revealing us as faultless; is heralded as Savior; and possesses endless glory and majesty, power and authority.

Coming Salvation and Judgment. Jude had wanted to write to the believers "about our amazing salvation we all participate in," for that is what we possess right now! Yet we are also waiting for our final salvation when Christ comes bearing eternal life. This is why Jude's theme of defending and contending for the faith is so important, for we are to preserve and persevere in our salvation until the end.

There's another reason: judgment. For along with his salvation, the Lord will bear judgment for all the ungodly. Jude reveals that God destroys those who are guilty of unbelief, give themselves to immorality, slander heavenly beings, and corrupt his church. Judgment makes the issue of false teaching that much more important, for such people sow seeds of division and doubt.

Which is why we're called to come alongside those who doubt their salvation, and offer Christ's saving work in order to snatch people from the fires of judgment.

Jude

Truth Worth Fighting For

[1]From Judah,[a] a loving servant[b] of Jesus, the Anointed One, and brother of James.[c] *I'm writing* to the chosen ones who are wrapped in the love of Father God—kept and guarded for[d] Jesus, the Messiah. [2]May God's mercy, peace, and love[e] cascade over you![f]

[3]Dearly loved friend, I was fully intending to write to you about our *amazing* salvation we all participate in, but felt the need instead to challenge you to vigorously defend and contend for[g] the beliefs that we cherish.[h] For God, *through the apostles,* has once for all entrusted these truths to his holy believers.

Warning Against False Teachers

[4]There have been some who have sneaked in among you unnoticed.[i] They

---

a 1 Or Jude. The Greek is *Judas*. This was a common Hebrew/Aramaic name during the time of Jesus, and there were two of the Twelve who had this name.

b 1 The Greek word *doulos* implies a close and lasting relationship to a master; love is implied.

c This James was the brother of our Lord Jesus. Jude is not asserting his family ties to Jesus but to James, as a sign of his humility. Instead of introducing himself as the half-brother of Jesus, he chose to describe himself simply as a "loving slave of Jesus and brother of James." Jude is not boasting of a physical commonality with Jesus but a spiritual relationship he has with the risen Christ. See Matthew 13:55, where he is named as a (half) brother of Jesus.

d 1 Or "by."

e 2 Jude adds the word *love* to the typical greeting of mercy and peace.

f 2 Or "be multiplied in you."

g 3 Or "Keep adding to the contest" or "Repeatedly participate fully in the race course."

h 3 Although the Greek here is "the faith" or "on behalf of the faith," it is clear that Jude is not speaking of faith as simply believing in God. The Christian faith encompasses the body of truth we receive from the inspired Word of God. It is possible that Jude wrote his letter after the death of Peter and was referring to 1 and 2 Peter, a few of Paul's early letters, or even Mark's gospel.

i 4 See Acts 20:29–30 and 2 Peter 2:1.

are depraved people whose judgment was prophesied in Scripture[a] a long time ago. They have perverted *the message of* God's grace into a license to commit immorality[b] and turn against[c] our only absolute Master,[d] our Lord Jesus Christ.

⁵I need to remind you, even though you are familiar with it all, that *the Lord Jesus*[e] saved his people out of Egypt but subsequently destroyed those who were guilty of unbelief.

⁶In the same way, there were heavenly messengers *in rebellion* who went outside their rightful domain of authority[f] and abandoned their appointed realms.[g] God bound them in everlasting chains and is keeping them in the dark abyss of the *netherworld* until the judgment of the great day.

⁷In a similar way, the cities of Sodom and Gomorrah and nearby towns[h]

---

a 4 Or "written." It is possible that Jude is referring not only to Old Testament prophecies but also to the New Testament book of 2 Peter.

b 4 Or "debauchery." See Romans 6:1 and Titus 2:11–14. The gospel of grace is beautiful to our ears. God's grace empowers and equips us to live in an ascended life so that we are not distracted or detoured by our former life of sin.

c 4 Or "deny."

d 4 Or "Sovereign (God)." They deny the authority, glory, and sovereignty of our Master (God) and our Lord Jesus Christ.

e 5 Some reliable manuscripts have "the Lord," while other very reliable early manuscripts have "Jesus." This translation, for the sake of clarity, includes both Lord and Jesus. This is an incredible reference of the preincarnate Jesus, who powerfully delivered the Hebrew people before he was even born.

f 6 Or "their own principality" or "their native state."

g 6 See Genesis 6:1–4 and 2 Peter 2:4–8. This episode is referring to angels who abandoned the heavenly realm to come to earth to have intercourse with women in order to corrupt the godly lineage of Seth. Cain had already gone into the darkness of sin, but the godly line of Seth would one day bring forth Noah, and from his seed (Shem), Jesus would eventually be born. The rebellious rank of angels mentioned here had sex with women who then gave birth to the Nephilim (mighty giants). Ancient references to this can be found in the writings of early Jewish writers, including Josephus and Philo of Alexandria, as well as early church fathers, such as Justin Martyr, Irenaeus, Clement of Alexandria, Ambrose of Milan, Athenagoras, Tertullian, Eusebius, Lactantius, Jerome, Augustine of Hippo, and Sulpicius Severus. All of them, along with the Septuagint, identified these "sons of God" as the offspring of angels. See also 1 Enoch 10. This sin was one of the significant causes for the flood.

h 7 This would include Admah and Zeboyim (Deuteronomy 29:23).

gave themselves to sexual immorality and the unnatural desire of different flesh.[a] Now they all serve as examples of those who experience the punishment of eternal fire.[b]

The Fate of Apostates

[8]In the same way, these sensual "dreamers" corrupt and pollute the natural realm, while on the other hand they reject the *spiritual* realms of governmental power and repeatedly scoff at heavenly glories.[c] [9]Even the archangel Michael,[d] when he was disputing with the Devil over the body of Moses,[e] dared not insult or slander him, but simply said, "The Lord Yahweh[f] rebuke you!"[g]

[10]These people insult anything they don't understand. They behave like

---

a 7 Or "strange flesh." This is homosexuality, but it includes any sexual deviation or immorality. In the pseudographical book The Testament of Naphtali, 3.3.4–5 refers to sexual relations between the women of Sodom and these fallen angels, called "Watchers." The Book of Jubilees makes mention of holy angels sent by God to punish the "Watchers." Second Enoch describes the people of Sodom as committing abominations such as pedophilia, sorcery, magic enchantments, and the worship of many gods. First Enoch 6–10 indicates there were two hundred of these "Watchers" who came to earth, lusting after the women of Sodom who had offspring (Nephilim) from their sexual relations with them. Both humanity and angels violated the boundaries God had set in place.

b 7 Jude gives us three examples from ancient history in verses 5–7, pointing to those who experienced wonderful privileges from God but terribly abused God's grace and so were punished. Sodom and Gomorrah was described as fertile, fruitful, "like the garden of the Lord" (Genesis 13:10). Each example cited (Israel's exodus, angels that sinned, and the cities of sexual perversion) serves as an example and a warning that God judges sin. There is an eternal punishment of fire awaiting all who refuse to hide themselves in the love and grace of God, which is expressed through Christ toward us.

c 8 Or "blaspheming reputations"; that is, angelic beings.

d 9 See Daniel 10:13, 21; 12:1; Revelation 12:7. Michael is one of the highest angelic messengers, who is seen as leading the angelic host in war against the Devil and his angels.

e 9 Moses' death is mentioned in Deuteronomy 34:5–6.

f 9 As translated from the Aramaic.

g 9 See 2 Peter 2:10–12. It is obvious here that Michael the archangel had a measure of respect for spiritual powers, even toward the Devil. A possible translation of the Greek word *epitimao* is "to hold in high regard" or "to respect." Most scholars believe that Jude is quoting from the book of *The Assumption of Moses*, as cited also by some church fathers (Clement of Alexandria and Origen).

irrational beasts by doing whatever they feel like doing.ᵃ Because they live by their animal instincts, they corrupt themselves and bring about their own destruction. ¹¹How terrible it is for them!ᵇ For they have followed in the steps of Cain.ᶜ They have abandonedᵈ themselves to Balaam's error because of their greedy pursuit of financial gain.ᵉ *And since they have rebelled like Korah rebelled,* they will experience the same fate of Korah and likewise perish.ᶠ

¹²These false teachers are like dangerous hidden reefs at your love feasts,ᵍ *lying in wait to shipwreck the immature.* They feast among you without reverence,ʰ having no shepherd but themselves.ⁱ They are clouds with no rain,ʲ swept along by the winds.ᵏ Like fruitless late-autumn treesˡ—twice dead,ᵐ barren, and plucked up by the roots! ¹³They are wild waves of the

---

a 10 There is an implication that they are like animals in heat, following their natural instincts.

b 11 Or "A curse is on them."

c 11 See Genesis 4:3-8. The way of Cain was to reject the blood sacrifice that God desired and instead offer the fruit of his own labors (works). False teachers will insist on adding something to the gospel, polluting it with human works.

d 11 Or "poured out (themselves)."

e 11 Balaam's error was an abuse of the prophetic gift for financial gain. See Numbers 22–24; 31:16.

f 11 See Numbers 16. Korah led 250 men in rebellions against the leadership of Moses. The earth opened up and swallowed Korah alive. In a similar way, the "things of this earth" enticed these false teachers and they would be "swallowed up" by their greed for what this world can offer. Jude gives us three illustrations of wicked men who did as they pleased and suffered greatly: Cain, Balaam, and Korah.

g 12 Love feasts! What a beautiful description of what our church gatherings are meant to be. We celebrate the love of Christ through our communion, worship, teaching, prophesying, and fellowship together in our love for one another.

h 12 See 1 Corinthians 11:17-22.

i 12 Or "shepherds who care for only themselves." The Aramaic is "They submit their souls to no one."

j 12 Rain in the Bible is often a symbol of revelatory teaching (Deuteronomy 32:2).

k 12 Both in Hebrew and in Aramaic, the word Jude would use for "winds" is *spirits.* "Swept along by the spirits."

l 12 Autumn trees are often quite stunning in beauty, but these false teachers are bearing no fruit. They have the appearance of being true, but there is no fruit connected to their lives and ministries.

m 12 They are dead in appearance and dead in reality—dead through and through.

sea, flinging out the foam of their shame and disgrace.[a] They are *misleading* like wandering stars,[b] for whom the complete darkness of eternal gloom has been reserved.[c]

Enoch's Prophecy

[14]Enoch, the seventh direct descendant from Adam,[d] prophesied of their doom[e] when he said, "Look! Here comes the Lord Yahweh[f] with his countless myriads of holy ones. [15]*He comes* to execute judgment against them all and to convict each one of them for their ungodly deeds and for all the terrible words that ungodly sinners have spoken against him."[g]

[16]These people are always complaining and never satisfied—finding fault with everyone. They follow their own evil desires and their mouths speak scandalous things. They *enjoy* using seductive flattery to manipulate others.[h]

A Call to Remain Faithful

[17]But you, *my* delightfully loved friends, remember the prophecies of the apostles of our Lord Jesus, the Anointed One. [18]They taught you, "In the last days[i] there will always be mockers, motivated by their own ungodly desires."[j] [19]These people cause divisions and are followers of their own natural instincts, devoid of *the life of* the Spirit.

---

a 13 The Aramaic is "They manifest their confusion."

b 13 Stars were seen as navigational tools for seamen. But these false teachers could not be depended on and would give disastrous guidance. The word *misleading* is found in the Aramaic.

c 13 This is an Hebraic expression that is meant to convey the place of future eternal punishment, the farthest away from God that anyone could ever be.

d 14 That would be Adam, Seth, Enosh, Kenan, Mahalalel, Jared, and Enoch.

e 14 Or "prophesied against them."

f 14 As translated from the Aramaic. The Greek can also be translated "The Lord has come (*proleptic aorist*)."

g 15 See 1 Enoch 1:9.

h 16 Or "admiring faces (of the rich) for their own (financial) gain."

i 18 The last days began at Pentecost and have continued for more than two thousand years. We have been living in the last days since the Holy Spirit was poured out. See Acts 2:17 and Hebrews 1:2.

j 17 See Acts 20:29; 1 Timothy 4:1; 2 Timothy 3:1–5; 2 Peter 3:2–3; 2 John 7.

[20]But you, *my* delightfully loved friends, constantly and progressively build yourselves up on the foundation of your most holy faith[a] by praying every moment in the Spirit.[b] [21]Fasten your hearts to the love of God and receive the mercy of our Lord Jesus Christ, who gives us eternal life.[c]

[22]Keep being compassionate to those who still have doubts,[d] [23]and snatch others out of the fire to save them. Be merciful over and over to them, but always couple your mercy with the fear of God. Be extremely careful to keep yourselves free from the pollutions of the flesh.[e]

[24]Now, to the one with enough power to prevent you from stumbling *into sin*[f] and bring you faultless before his glorious presence to stand before him with ecstatic delight, [25]to the only God our Savior, through our Lord Jesus Christ, be *endless* glory and majesty, great power and authority—from before he created time, now, and throughout all the ages of eternity. Amen![g]

---

a 20 Or "faithfulness."

b 20 Paul uses this phrase "praying in the Spirit" to refer to praying in tongues. See Romans 8:26; Ephesians 6:18; 1 Corinthians 14:15. It can also mean "Pray as led by the Spirit," "Pray in the Spirit's realm," or "Pray by means of/power of the Spirit."

c 21 Or "By constantly and progressively building each other up on the foundation of your most holy faith, and by praying every moment in the Spirit's power, you will keep yourselves in the love of God, awaiting the mercy of our Lord Jesus, who gives eternal life."

d 22 Or "Show mercy to those who are still undecided."

e 23 Or "hating even the garment ('snake skin' or 'coating') of the pollution of the flesh (the natural realm)." In other words, we do all we can to bring others to Christ, but not at the expense of becoming like them in ignoring sin. Jude, in closing, gives us seven commands: 1) Keep building up your inner life on the foundation of faith; 2) Pray in the Holy Spirit; 3) Fasten your life to the love of God; 4) Receive more mercy from our Lord Jesus Christ; 5) Have compassion on the wavering; 6) Share the gospel with those who are lost; 7) Hate any compromise that will stain our lives.

f 24 The Greek word *aptaistos*, an hapax legomenon, is translated in classical Greek as "to keep from harm."

g 25 The Aramaic adds, "The end of the letter of the apostle Judah, the brother of Jacob and Joseph."

A Word About The Passion Translation

The message of God's story is timeless; the Word of God doesn't change. But the methods by which that story is communicated should be timely; the vessels that steward God's Word can and should change.

One of those timely methods and vessels is Bible translations. Bible translations are both a gift and a problem. They give us the words God spoke through his servants, but words can become very poor containers for revelation—they leak! Over time the words change from one generation to the next. Meaning is influenced by culture, background, and many other details. You can imagine how differently the Hebrew authors of the Old Testament saw the world three thousand years ago!

There is no such thing as a truly literal translation of the Bible, for there is not an equivalent language that perfectly conveys the meaning of the biblical text except as it is understood in its original cultural and linguistic setting. Therefore, a translation can be a problem. The problem, however, is solved when we seek to transfer meaning, and not merely words, from the original text to the receptor language.

The Passion Translation is new, heart-level translation (from Hebrew, Greek, and Aramaic manuscripts), which expresses God's fiery heart of love to this generation, merging the emotion and life-changing truth of God's Word.

You will notice at times we've italicized certain words or phrases. These highlighted portions are not in the original Hebrew, Aramaic, and Greek manuscripts, but are implied from the context. We've made these implications explicit for the sake of narrative clarity and to better convey the meaning of God's Word. This is a common practice by mainstream translations, including the New American Standard Bible and King James Version.

We've also chosen to translate certain names in their original Hebrew or Greek form to better convey their cultural meaning and significance. For instance, it is unfortunate that translations of the Bible have substituted

Miriam with Mary and Jacob with James. Both Greek and Aramaic leave the Hebrew names in their original form. Therefore this translation uses their correct cultural names, Miriam and Jacob, throughout.

God longs to have his Word expressed in every language in a way that would unlock the passion of his heart. Our goal is to trigger inside every reader an overwhelming response to the truth of the Bible, unfolding the deep mysteries of the Scriptures in the love language of God, the language of the heart.

We pray and trust this version of God's Word will kindle in you a burning, passionate desire for him and his heart, while impacting the church for years to come!

About the Translator

Dr. Brian Simmons is known as a passionate lover of God. After a dramatic conversion to Christ, Brian knew that God was calling him to go to the unreached people of the world and present the gospel of God's grace to all who would listen. With his wife, Candice, and their three children, he spent nearly eight years in the tropical rain forest of the Darien Province of Panama as a church planter, translator, and consultant. Brian was involved in the Paya-Kuna New Testament translation project. He studied linguistics and Bible translation principles with New Tribes Mission. After their ministry in the jungle, Brian was instrumental in planting a thriving church in New England (USA), and now travels full time as a speaker and Bible teacher. He has been happily married to Candice for over forty-two years and is known to boast regularly of his children and grandchildren. Brian and Candice may be contacted at:

Facebook.com/passiontranslation
Twitter.com/tPtBible

For more information about the translation project or any of Brian's books, please visit:

thePassionTranslation.com
StairwayMinistries.org

thePassionTranslation.com